# Hg2 Marrakech

A Hedonist's guide to
# Marrakech

BY Paul Sullivan
PHOTOGRAPHY Paul Sullivan

A Hedonist's guide to Marrakech

Managing director – Tremayne Carew Pole
Series editor – Catherine Blake
Production – Navigator Guides
Design – P&M Design
Typesetting – Dorchester Typesetting
Repro – PDQ Digital Media Solutions
Printers – Printed in Italy by Printer Trento srl
PR – Ann Scott Associates
Publisher – Filmer Ltd
Additional photography – Tremayne Carew Pole
Additional text – Tremayne Carew Pole

Email – info@ahedonistsguideto.com
Website – www.ahedonistsguideto.com

First Published in the United Kingdom in 2004 by
Filmer Ltd
47 Filmer Road,
London SW6 7JJ

ISBN – 0 9547878 0 3

# Hg2 Marrakech

## CONTENTS

# How to…

A Hedonist's guide to… is broken down into easy to use sections: Sleep, Eat, Drink, Snack, Party, Culture, Shop, Play and Info. In each of these sections you will find detailed reviews and photographs.

At the front of the book you will find an introduction to the city and an overview map, followed by introductions to the four main areas and more detailed maps. On each of these maps you will see the places that we have reviewed, laid out by section, highlighted on the map with a symbol and a number. To find out about a particular place, simply turn to the relevant section where all entries are listed alphabetically.

Alternatively, browse through a specific section (i.e. Eat) until you find a restaurant that you like the look of. Next to your choice will be a small coloured dot – each colour refers to a particular area of the city – then simply turn to the relevant map to discover the location.

# Updates

Due to the lengthy publishing process and shelf lives of books it is very difficult to keep travel guides up to date – new restaurants, bars and hotels open up all the time, while others simply fade away or just go out of style. What we can offer you are free updates – simply log onto our website www.ahedonistsguideto.com or www.hg2.net and enter your details, answer a relevant question to provide proof of purchase and you will be entitled to free updates for a year from the date that you sign up. This will enable you to have all the relevant information at your finger tips whenever you go away.

In order to help us with this any comments that you might have, or recommendations that you would like to see in the guide in future, please feel free to email us at info@ahedonistsguideto.com.

# The concept

A Hedonist's guide to... is designed to appeal to a more urbane and stylish traveller. The kind of traveller who is interested in gourmet food, elegant hotels and seriously chic bars – the traveller who feels the need to explore, shop and pamper themselves away from the madding crowd.

Our aim is to give you the inside knowledge of the city, to make you feel like a well-heeled, sophisticated local and to take you to the most fashionable places in town to rub shoulders with the local glitterati.

In today's world work rules our life, weekends away are few and far between, and when we do go away we want to have the most fun and relaxation possible with the minimum of stress. This guide is all about maximizing time. Everywhere is photographed, so before you go you know exactly what you are getting into; choose a restaurant or bar that suits you and your demands.

We pride ourselves on our independence and our integrity. We eat in all the restaurants, drink in all the bars and go wild in the nightclubs – all totally incognito. We charge no one for the privilege for appearing in the guide, every place is reviewed and included at our discretion.

We feel cities are best enjoyed by soaking up the atmosphere and the vibrancy: wander the streets, indulge in some retail relaxation therapy, re-energize yourself with a massage and then get ready to eat like a king and party hard on the stylish local scene.

We feel that it is important for you to explore a city on your own terms, while the places reviewed provide definitive coverage in our eyes; one's individuality can never be wholly accounted for. Whatever you do we can assure you that you will have an unforgettable weekend.

# Marrakech

One of the most talked-about cities in recent years, Marrakech has become a haven for those interested in design, shopping and the naturally exotic. The centrepiece in what is widely regarded as North Africa's adventure playground, it has brought international sophistication to this dusty, dry corner of the world.

Despite almost 50 years of French occupation and a brisk trade in tourism, the city has maintained a sense of mystery and old-world charm not found anywhere else so close to Europe.

The city was initially founded in 1062 by the Almoravids, a Berber tribe who planted the palm trees and erected the distinctive walls, which still stand proudly today. Over the next thousand years it came under the rule of various tribes and peoples from the Almohads (1147–1289), the Merenids (1276–1554), the Saadians (1549–1668) and between 1912 and 1956 the French.

It was during the Swinging Sixties, however, that Marrakech gained its major bohemian appeal, as the likes of Yves St Laurent, The Beatles, The Rolling Stones and Jean-Paul Getty all came to hang out here. The trend continued as increasing numbers of style-conscious ex-pats came to the city to invest their money and design ideas, thus creating the mix of ancient tradition and modern chic that epitomizes the place today. The eruption of sophisticated *riads*, influenced and inspired by Islamic art but also by practical necessity, has drawn visitors to the luxurious, photogenic interiors – introducing a hotel experience almost unparalleled elsewhere in the world.

So what does Marrakech have to offer?

The streets of the Medina provide a rare insight into the lives of ordinary Marrakchi; they transport one back in time and contrast markedly with the relative sophistication and Westernization of Gueliz and the newer parts of the city.

Shopping, the likes of which you never thought possible.

The perfect day might involve wandering the ancient streets of the Medina in the morning, soaking up the bustling, ramshackle, pre-industrial atmosphere. You may then discover, behind an unlikely old door, an über-trendy restaurant, just perfect for a spot of lunch.

Afterwards, you could check out the souks or head to Gueliz for a coffee and some boutique shopping.

In the evening it might be nice to indulge in the full grandeur of the Moroccan dining experience at one of the palace restaurants, then take a refreshing mint tea at a café on the Jemaa el Fna and marvel at the nocturnal madness that has been unfolding in a similar way for the last thousand years.

Finally, you might head back to your quiet, comfortable *riad* for a sound night's sleep, full of exotic Arabian dreams.

If you feel the need to get out of the city then there is a wealth of adventure open to you. The High Atlas Mountains are a mere 40km from Marrakech, so an hour's taxi ride will see you firmly ensconced among them. Here you can ride, trek, ski or simply soak up the purity of the air and inhale the natural aromas. In spring, wild flowers cover the mountainsides, while in autumn the smells of the fruit harvest assail the senses.

A little further away you can begin to explore the edges of the Sahara. This magnificent, dry desert offers stunning scenery unlike anything else. The beautiful sand dunes and rock formations will take your breath away, while you can also make the most of this unique opportunity to see some of the people who live here.

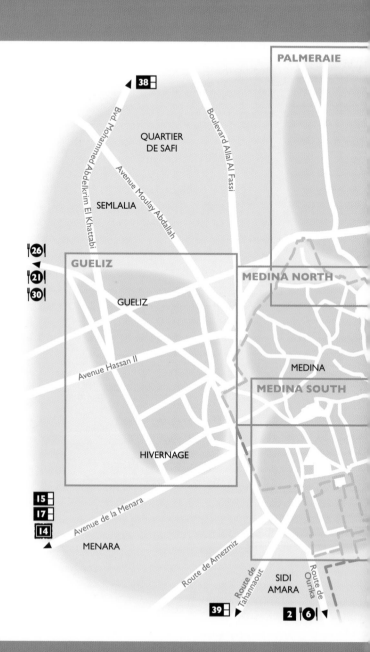

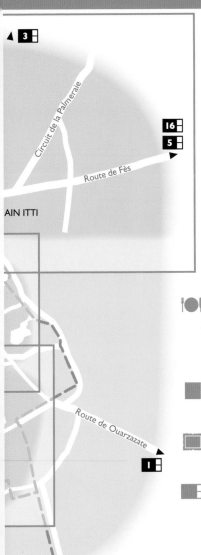

AIN ITTI

Circuit de la Palmeraie

Route de Fès

Route de Ouarzazate

0    0.5    1km

## 🍽 EAT

6.  Bô - Zin
21. Le Jardin des Arts
26. La Madrage de St. Tropez
30. Pizzeria Niagara

## DRINK

2.  Bô - Zin

## CULTURE

14. Menara Gardens

## SLEEP

1.  Amanjena
3.  Caravanserai
5.  Dar Bab Jenny
15. Kasbah Agafay
16. Kasbah des Roses
17. Kasbah du Toubkal
38. Tichka Salam
39. Tigmi

# The Medina (North)

It's within the dense, claustrophobic walls of the ancient Medina that the magic and mystery of Morocco reveal themselves alongside the everyday hustle and bustle. It's where the majority of visitors to Marrakech will spend their time.

The non-stop parade of street traders, cart-pulling donkeys, sweating artisans, blind beggars, playful children and assorted mysterious figures seems as if it could have been frozen in time a thousand years ago – and in many ways it has.

For some, the Medina is initially overwhelming, although a few hours should be enough to help anyone relax into the natural – if hectic – pulse.

The biggest draws are the Jemaa El Fna and the souks, as well as an assortment of historic sights such as the Koutoubia Mosque and the Ben Youssef Medersa, but one of the most memorable adventures is simply to succumb to the vicissitudes of the maze.

Strolling down nameless street after nameless street (the locals will always guide you back on track if you stray too far or wander where

you shouldn't), you will discover sights, smells and a unique way of living that will leave permanent impressions upon your imagination.

The Medina saw the start of the *riad* culture – small, intimate hotels, housed in traditional courtyarded buildings, offering tranquillity and solace from the bustling alleyways and souks. There are several wonderful examples of these, notably Riad Farnatchi, Riad El Fenn and Tchaikana.

The Medina's policy regarding alcohol is not as relaxed as elsewhere in Marrakech, as it is the Old City and home to some of the most important mosques. Here alcohol can only be found in the hotel bars, the likes of the Jardins de la Koutoubia or in the many restaurants. There are some fabulous restaurants to visit, set in stunning old buildings, where you are seated in a courtyard beside gurgling fountains, while rose petals are strewn over your table – opulence and romance are the bywords here. While you are in Marrakech, visits to Le Tobsil, Dar Moha or Dar Marjana are highly recommended.

Leaving the best until last, the Medina's greatest draw is the souk. These small stalls clustered together by trade are found in warren-like alleys that lead from the Jemaa al Fna. This, for some, is the essence of the Marrakech experience. Haggle over a pair of highly sequinned *baboush*, trade essential cooking tips with the spice merchants or merely let the sights, sounds and smells wash over you.

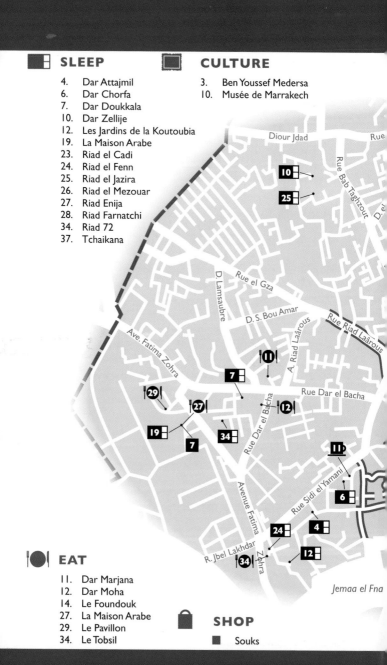

Diour Jdad

Rue

Rue Bab Taghzout

D. el

Rue el Gza

D. Lamsaubre

D. S. Bou Amar

A. Riad Laârous

Rue Riad Laârous

Ave. Fatima Zohra

Rue Dar el Bacha

Rue Dar el Bacha

Avenue Fatima Zohra

Rue Sidi el Yamani

R. Jbel Lakhdar

Zohra

Jemaa el Fna

# The Medina (North)   local map

■ **DRINK**

   7.   La Maison Arabe

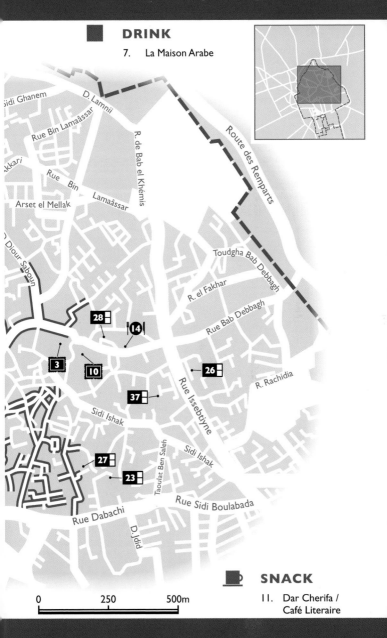

■ **SNACK**

   11.   Dar Cherifa /
          Café Literaire

0        250        500m

# The Medina (South)

The southern half of the Medina is somewhat less hectic than the north, while there are still the twisiting and turning *derbs* and alleyways, the workshops and souks are less obvious. This is more of a residential area, seemingly more affluent than the northern half.

Like the north it is filled with interesting sights and sounds. The Bahia Palace, the Saadian Tombs, the Royal Palace and the Agdal Gardens draw visitors interested in the history and architecture of the city. Then there is the Koutoubia, visible from virtually all points in the city as well as the meeting-place that is the Jemaa El Fna, for most the central point of navigation within the Medina.

Some of Marrakech's finest *riads* and hotels are found here; the legendary Mamounia, the luxurious Villa des Orangers and the elegant, calm Dar Cigognes. They epitomize the style and design with which the city has become synonymous and are dedicated to contemplative relaxation.

The contrast between life inside and outside the Medina is palpable. Within the walls of the old city time stands still, little has changed, motorbikes have replaced donkeys as the favoured form of transport,

cars are few and far between, meat for sale is unlikely to be refridgerated and old women sell fresh herbs from boxes on the road side. While outside life is very much in the 21st century: McDonalds, TV and traffic jams form part of everyday life – a world full of modern conveniences.

Life in the Medina is so far removed from our day-to-day experience back home that staying in it is a real breath of fresh air.

Indulging in a hammam and gommage is one thing that all visitors to Marrakech should do. A weekly cleansing ritual for locals, many of whom live without showers and baths, is essential to personal hygiene. The local hammams can often be daunting places for a stranger but everyone is incredibly welcoming and someone will guide you through the whole process. In this part of town is the Bains de Marrakech – an upmarket and relatively expensive spa – if basic native haunts aren't up your street this is definitely the place to rejuvenate and de-stress.

## DRINK

4.   Churchill's Piano Bar
9.   The Piano Bar

## EAT

1.   Al Baraka
9.   Chez Chegouni
13.  El Marrakchi
15.  Les Jardins de la Koutoubia
16.  L'Italien
20.  Les Jardins de la Medina
22.  Jemaa el Fna
24.  Ksar el Hamra
28.  Mamounia Moroccain
32.  Riad Tamsna
33.  Les Terraces de l'Alhambra
36.  Trois Palmiers

## CULTURE

1.   Badii Palace
2.   Bahia Palace
4.   Jemaa el Fna
5.   Koutoubia Mosque
6.   Saadian Tombs
7.   Dar Tiskiwin
11.  Agdal Gardens
13.  Mamounia Gardens

0      250      500m

# Gueliz/Hivernage

Gueliz – the New City – was constructed in 1913, soon after the French took power. The broad, European-style avenues and boulevards convey a sense of space, order and cleanliness a world away from the intricate chaos of the Medina.

This Westernized quarter – which borders Hivernage, virtually an extension of Gueliz – is home to the financial and business community: here lies the power. This is borne out by the continued growth in the number of international business hotels, expensive restaurants and chic bars in the area.

For the visitor, however, Gueliz/Hivernage is best for its nightlife. Home to the majority of the city's finest bars and clubs, this is where it all goes on after dinner. The bar at Le Comptoir is possibly the finest in Marrakech, whereas the roof terrace at the Montecristo offers star-gazing and hookah pipes. The Paradise, Theatro and Jad Mahal night-clubs all offer similarly cheesy music, expensive drinks and an array of beautiful women who need little persuasion to come over and join you.

Gueliz is not only known for its nightlife but also for some of the

city's best restaurants, cafés and art galleries. The restaurant scene is particularly vibrant; dinner at the wildly opulent Jad Mahal is an exercise in style and people-watching, while a trip to La Trattoria di Giancarlo offers unparalleled Italian food in intimate but extraordinary surroundings.

There are plenty of shopping options as well, for hipsters and traditionalists alike, and strolling casually along Mohammed V and its various arteries can provide pleasant respite from the bartering intensity of the souks. Galleries show new Moroccan art, clothes designers work on contemporary takes on traditional clothing and antique shops give you the opportunity to furnish your very own *riad*.

Admittedly for the sightseer there is not as much as in many other cities, but it's perfectly possible to spend a memorable day or evening (or both) in Gueliz, taking a breakfast at Vittoria or Les Negoçiants, visiting the Majorelle Gardens, or the central market (Marché Central) and then heading to a restaurant or bar come night-time.

A *petit* taxi between the Medina and Gueliz costs around 10dh and takes around 5 minutes – what have you got to lose?

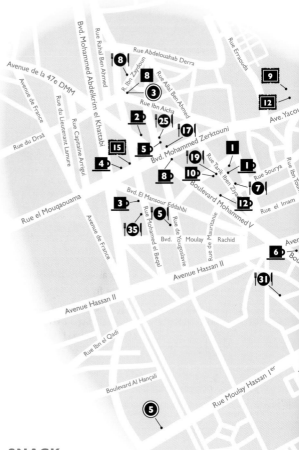

## SNACK

# Gueliz   local map

0      250      500m

## ▣ DRINK

1.  Bodega
3.  La Casa
5.  Le Comptoir
6.  Jad Mahal
8.  Montecristo

## 🍽 EAT

2.  Al Fassia
3.  Alizia
4.  L' Amandier
5.  La Bagatelle
7.  Catanzaro
8.  Les Cepages
10. Le Comptoir
17. Le Jacaranda
18. Jad Mahal
19. Les Jardins de Geliz
25. Le Lounge
31. Puerto Banus
35. La Trattoria di Giancarlo

## ◉ PARTY

1.  Diamant Noir
2.  Jad Mahal
3.  Montecristo
5.  Paradise
6.  Theatro
7.  VIP
8.  Es Saadi Casino

## ▤ CULTURE

9.  Musée d'Art Islamique
12. Majorelle Gardens
15. Colisée

# La Palmeraie

A 15-minute drive outside the old city, the area is famous for its eponymous trees and for the wealth of luxury accommodation (public and private) that exists here.

The Palmeraie is a dusty and arid suburb of Marrakech, created without any apparent structure or form. It is home to spacious hotel complexes, including some wonderfully opulent oases of decadence, and some of the finest golf courses that Morocco has to offer.

The level and comfort of the accommodation available makes La Palmeraie an attractive option for those seeking solace from hurly-burly city life without being too far removed from it. The ramshackle, old-world charm of Les Deux Tours and Ayniwen promise exclusivity and privacy, while pampering your every whim. Then there is the unparalleled luxury of the Amanjena, the North African branch of the Aman resorts, that provides a choice of lavish pavilions built around an enormous reflecting pool and a range of fantastic restaurants and decadent services. The newly built Ksar Char-Bagh offers luxury and intimacy to rival, but on a smaller scale.

In terms of activity, the Palmeraie offers a lot – the Palmeraie Golf Palace has an excellent golf course, a good riding stable and a spa to enjoy after your exertions. Additional challenging golf courses are found at Amelkis and the Royal Golf Club, which host national and international tournaments. Camel treks can be arranged around the circuit, giving tourists a chance to enjoy that 'authentic' desert experience – or one can just wander among the palm groves and admire the desert landscape.

In short, unless you're staying or planning to stay in the Palmeraie, fancy a round of golf or want an insight into the lives of the rich and famous, there is little reason to pay a visit. If you are staying here expect wonderful peace, luxury and exclusivity.

**EAT**

23  Ksar Char-Bagh

**DRINK**

10.  Zanzibar

**PARTY**

4.  New Feeling

**SNACK**

13.  Sunset

**SLEEP**

2.  Ayniwen
9.  Dar Liqama
11.  Les Deux Tours
14.  Jnane Tamsna
18.  Ksar Char-Bagh
40.  Topkapi

Route de Fès

0    0.5    1km

# sleep...

If there's one thing Marrakech isn't short of, it's accommodation. Running the gamut from scruffy budget dorms and backpacker hostels to anonymous corporate hotels and ultra-luxury villas, the city ensures it caters for every type of traveller.

In the last ten years the Medina has seen an explosion in the number of *riad* conversions. A *riad* is a traditional Moroccan house built around a central, internal courtyard which normally features a garden with a fountain in the centre. From the centre four paths lead off to salons on the ground floor, providing relaxation and eating areas, while the upper floors contain the sleeping quarters with a balcony running around the central atrium. At roof level, most of the *riads* have a terrace, which is a wonderful place to sit and sip an evening drink. What started with French ex-pats has become an international phenomenon, with many townhouses being snapped up and transformed into stylish *maison d'hôtes*, infused with chic and abundant charm.

The Medina's *riads* are often intimate, elegantly decorated and, increasingly, the essence of Moroccan hip. Not only do they give relief from the heat during the hot summers and tranquillity away from the hustle and bustle of the surrounding alleyways and souks, but they also provide also fabulous views over the Medina rooftops and a glimpse into the lives of the ordinary Marrakchi. Some of the better examples of these in the Medina are Tchaikana, Villa des Orangers and Riad Enija.

Through a process of natural selection, the more secluded, luxurious villas and hotels are located in Palmeraie, a desert suburb of Marrakech 15 minutes' drive from the centre of town. Here high-end, design-led houses are spread out, accessible via a maze of winding dirt tracks, shaded beneath the palm trees that give the district its name. Ayniwen and Les Deux Tours are two of the quieter places to stay, tucked away behind high walls and gated entrances with oases of green surrounding their azure swimming pools, their décor somewhat reminiscent of bygone eras.

No city is complete without its share of anonymous corporate hotels – which are mainly crowded together in the Gueliz district, the New Town. These large office-like edifices, which are not included here, are close to the bars, restaurants and nightclubs but as a rule lack the charm and intimacy of the Medina's riads, and number amongst them some of the more prevalent international chains. We see no reason to include them here when there are so many memorable and stylish options.

We have included, however, a few of the über-sophisticated hotels lying just outside the city limits. The Berber-led Caravanserai and Tigmi revel in their simplicity while the provision of luxury and service at the Amanjena is without parallel elsewhere in Marrakech.

It's worth noting that, wherever you stay, you should book ahead in peak seasons – especially if you are opting for the smaller places. Also, rates change according to season. Since different places have different interpretations of these seasonal periods (and some recognize seasons that others don't, such as a 'middle season'), we have listed the lowest 'low-season' price for a double room up to the highest 'high-season' price for a suite.

**Our top ten hotels in Marrakech are:**

1. Riad El Fenn
2. Ksar Char-Bagh
3. Villa des Orangers
4. Riad Farnatchi
5. Riad El Cadi
6. Riad Enija
7. Les Deux Tours
8. Dar les Cigognes
9. Jnane Tamsna
10. Tchaikana

**Our top five for style are:**

1. Ksar Car-Bagh
2. Les Deux Tours
3. Amanjena
4. Riad El Fenn
5. Caravanserai

**Our top five for atmosphere are:**

1. Kasbah Agafay
2. Ksar Char-Bagh
3. Riad El Fenn
4. Riad El Cadi
5. Jnane Tamsna

**Our top five for location are:**

1. Villa des Orangers
2. Riad El Cadi
3. Riad El Fenn
4. Riad Enija
5. Les Jardins de la Koutoubia

**Amanjena, Route de Ouarzazate, Km 12.**
Tel: 0 44 40 33 53 www.amanresorts.com
Rates: 8,500–28,000dh

They don't come much more exclusive than this. Part of the Aman Group – reckoned to be one of the foremost luxury hotel chains in the world – it's a have-to-see-it-to-believe-it place, a kind of traditional Moroccan palace (with Asian overtones) set on the outskirts of Marrakech. The dusty pink walls enclose a vast tract of even dustier land with postcard-perfect reflective pools, around which are set 41 rose-toned pavilions, six two-storey *maisons* and one fabulous suite. The rooms themselves are a wonder to behold, imaginatively styled at great expense with flair and panache; needless to say the Amanjena offers every kind of exclusive facility and service you could ever need (or imagine)

– from swimming pools and gardens, private pools to personal butlers, a series of boutiques, an extensive spa, two restaurants, tennis courts and a fitness centre. Golfers should also note that the resort is right next door to two of the city's three main courses. All you need to qualify for all this is the right expense account.

**Style 10, Atmosphere 8, Location 7**

**Ayniwen, Tafrata, Circuit de la Palmeraie, Palmeraie.**
Tel: 0 44 32 96 84/85 www.dar-ayniwen.com
Rates: 1,900–5,400dh

Ayniwen is the kind of place that makes it into *Condé Nast Traveller* Hot List and attracts reclusive celebrities such as Monica Bellucci. Built on two hectares of parkland in the Palmareie, the main house has a Romanesque grandeur and the opulence of an 18th-century palace – yet it was constructed as a family house as recently as the 1980s and opened up to the public just a couple of years ago. The four suites in the house look

out onto lush gardens, which enclose a pool and three additional private villas (also suites). Much importance is placed on catering to each guest's individual needs, so that you feel you are living in your own home or that of a friend. Décor is deliberately old-fashioned with an emphasis on local materials and lots of impressive imported antiques, which overwhelm all the mod-cons. Rooms and bathrooms are often huge and have a welcoming, lived-in feel, and although you feel like you are part of a large house party, intimacy and privacy is complete. Stephan, son of the original owners the Abtan family, lives in a separate house nearby and is on call to make sure all whims are fully catered for.

Style 8, Atmosphere 9, Location 7

**Caravanserai, 264 Ouled Ben Rahmoune.**
Tel: 0 44 30 03 02/283 www.caravanserai.com
Rates: 730–4,200dh

If it wasn't for the odd uniformed man loitering casually at the door and the occasional expensive car parked outside, you might mistake Caravanserei for any other traditional village house – from the outside. The 150-year-old building has been renovated in spectacularly authentic fashion and constructed to fit in seamlessly with its surroundings. Those surroundings happen to be a tiny Arabic village several miles outside Marrakech, a location intended to bring an authentic and rural Morocco to your doorstep. As nondescript as the outside may be, the inside is indescribably wondrous thanks to designer Charles Boccara, who has done his good reputation no harm by helping to create such a magical space. The 12 suites and five standard rooms (four doubles, one single) – inevitably breathtaking – are arranged around a courtyard dominated by a pool. Flanking the pool is a cosy restaurant/bar area on one side and a memorable designer garden on the other. There's a Moroccan and French menu, and terraces with stunning views of the Atlas and the Palmeraie. Staff float around noiselessly, soft music massages and impossibly perfect salons offer respite from the sun. It doesn't get much better than this.

**Style 9/10, Atmosphere 9, Location 6**

Dar Attajmil can be found along the meandering Rue Laksour, just next to a small artisan's workshop tucked in the corner. The place is run by charming Italian fashionista Lucrezia Mutti. With just four rooms, it's one of the smaller *riads* around, but what it

lacks in space and size it makes up for with its feeling of intimacy and chic design. The subtle smell of incense hangs over the splendid central courtyard and the nooks and crannies of the maze-like interior, which have been lovingly embellished with tasteful ornamentation. The rooms are on the poky side but are superbly kitted out with various takes on the Moroccan style and subtle mixes of antique and contemporary furnishings. The floral roof terrace is excellent, boasting an intimate *hammam* and spa (open to the public, but reservations essential: see page 184), where massages, skin treatments and face masks are all available. Extra services include a fashion boutique (which sells Lucrezia's own designer fashion label) and classes (from traditional Moroccan cooking to vegetable printing). This is an especially good place for women travelling alone.

**Style 8, Atmosphere 8, Location 8**

**Dar Bab Jenny, Ouled Hassoune, Route de Fes, 12km.**
Tel: 0 44 32 98 58 www.darbabjenny.com
Rates: 2,300–6,900dh

Bab Jenny was opened to the public a few years ago after the owner decided that she could do more with her capacious home than just invite her pals over now and again. The space is big enough to feature extensive gardens, tennis and basketball courts, an enormous swimming pool, a main house with five rooms and a separate palatial suite at the back of the house. It has a more open, breezy and down-to-earth feeling than many similar places, which comes no doubt from the intimate service. The main house is decorated in Moroccan style but has lots of natural light and plenty of salon spaces for relaxing, dining and watching TV. There's also a traditional bread-baking stove in the garden and a *hammam*. The master-suite is surely the *coup de grâce* with a sumptuous four-poster bed and a ridiculously luxurious bath you could launch a small ship into — although, of course, it doesn't come cheap.

Style 8, Atmosphere 8, Location 7

**Dar Chorfa, 6 Derb Chorfa Lakbir, Mouassine, Medina.**
Tel: 0 44 44 30 05 www.riadchorfa.com
Rates: 400–1,200dh

Dar Chorfa is located down a winding alley just off the Rue Mouassine (follow the signs to the Dar Cherifa Literary Café – it's just next door). It offers nine rooms set around an elegant courtyard, all eccentrically designed by owner and architect Bay J.B. Douceet-Bon, who opened the place just a couple of years ago. The touches he has bestowed range from the tasteful and bizarre to the interesting and occasionally cheesy (romantic paintings of wild horses anyone?). There are winding stairways, delectably contoured *tadelakt* bathrooms, architectual plans on the walls around the first floor, idiosyncratic pottery in the rooms, Herb Ritts photos, and a risqué blend of colours and shapes, all of which create a charmingly disorderly feel. Although the rooms have names more suited to the racing stables (Naughty Boy and Boite A Biscuit), the courtyard is charming and features a reflective pool, and the very reasonable prices make it a definite bargain.

Style 7, Atmosphere 8, Location 8

**Dar Doukkala, 83 Arset Aouzal, Bab Doukkala, Medina.**
Tel: 0 44 38 34 44 www.dardoukkala.com
Rates: 1,600–3,600dh

Dar Doukkala, named after its ancient neighbourhood, might not be much to look at from the outside – literally just a plain door at the end of an alley – but inside it is heart-breakingly gorgeous. It didn't open until January 2003, so is one of the newer kids on the block, but its reputation has spread quickly. The six rooms (recently expanded from four) unfurl organically around two floors connected by a majestic red and white stairwell. Designer Jean-Luc Lemée has transformed the place into a feast of art-

deco curves and madcap orientalism. Things to 'ooh' and 'aah' at include freestanding baths the length of submarines, cool Plexiglas furnishings and stunningly curvaceous fireplaces. The rooms (which include two suites) are all immaculately presented and have different themes. There are also a couple of salons, a shaded patio, a *hammam*, a small swimming pool and two terraces with views over the Medina.

**Style 8, Atmosphere 8, Location 8**

**Dar les Cigognes, 108 rue de Berima, Medina.**
Tel: 0 44 38 27 40 www.lescigognes.com
Rates: 1,300–2,500dh

Situated a *baboush*-throw away from the Badii Palace, Les Cigognes is a former 17th-century merchant's townhouse that has been renovated (with the help of star architect Charles Boccara) into a stylish boutique guesthouse. An elegant court-yard (featuring the obligatory citrus trees and gurgling fountain) is the centrepiece, symbolizing a peaceful ambience that is immediately apparent. Around the central courtyard subtle public spaces (dining room, library, salon, washrooms, alcoves) are gathered; although it's the rooms that really let the hipness hang out. There are 11 of them – including seven suites, a '*grande chambre*' and a '*chambre luxe*' – all with their own take on Moorish architectural and decorative traditions, and all with en-suite bathrooms with bath and shower facilities. Six of the suites have been recently added in an adjoining house, as well as two more sitting areas, a handicrafts boutique, a *hammam*, a small kitchen and a planted courtyard. A wonderful roof terrace is overlooked by the eponymous storks. Staff are incredibly friendly and helpful.

**Style 8, Atmosphere 8, Location 9**

**Dar Liqama, Douar Abiad, Palmeraie.**
Tel: 0 44 33 16 97 www.luxurypropertyrentals.com
Rates: 2,250–3,650dh

Some places just seem to have it all, and Dar Liqama is one of them. Comprising of two different, traditionally built houses – the stunning eight-room 'Liqama' and, right next door, the smaller but equally impressive four-room 'Louisa' – this exclusive Palmeraie resort doesn't leave much off the menu. Aside from the beautifully decorated rooms, facilities include a cooking school (in October and November: the owners run the interna-

tionally renowned Rhodes School of Cuisine), a billiard room, a dedicated wine cellar, a projector movie room, *hammam* and spa, tennis courts, swimming pool (which incorporates a children's pool) and gardens. Guests in both houses share all facilities (though the pools and gardens in each place are regarded as private to each house) and also enjoy suite-sized standard rooms as well as palatial suites and master bedrooms. As if things couldn't get any more romantic, there is a nifty Berber tent on the roof for stargazing or watching sunsets over the Palmeraie. It's also one of the few places with disabled access.

**Style 8, Atmosphere 8, Location 7**

**Dar Zellije, 46 Derb Ihihane, Sidi Ben Slimane, Medina.**
Tel: 0 44 38 26 27 www.marrakech-riads.net
Rates: 1,000dh

Dar Zellije has a special place among Marrakech's *riads* since it was one of the first local houses to be restored and converted into a guesthouse, thus kick-starting the *riad* boom. Previous guests include Jean Paul Gaultier, the wife of the last Shah of Iran and various ambassadors. The man behind the masterplan is Abdeletif Aït Ben Abdallah, the famed owner of Marrakech Riads: apparently he looked at more than 6,000 places before settling on this one. The house encapsulates his mission to present *mai-*

*son d'hôtes* as a cultural experience, i.e. leaving them as much as possible in their original state to showcase their ornamentation. In contrast with many other 'designer' spots, Zellije is a Spartan affair with any gaps in the 17th-century detailing left bare instead of being restored by modern artisans. This results in an unfinished feel, exacerbated by the simple furnishings, which encourage austerity. But the fine stucco detailing, cedarwood ceilings, decorated doors and eponymous tiling are the big draw, as well, of course, as the fine hospitality and four comfortable rooms.

**Style 8, Atmosphere 9, Location 7**

**Les Deux Tours, Douar Abiad, Circuit de la Palmeraie de Marrakesh (Municipalité An-Nakhil), Palmaraie.**
Tel: 0 44 32 95 25/26/27 www.les-deuxtours.com
Rates: 1,750–4,000dh

Introduced by two distinctively quirky mud towers at the side of a raw dirt track in La Palmeraie, Les Deux Tours is one of Marrakech's most well-known properties. It was designed by the one and only Charles Boccara, and nowhere is his imaginative flair more evident than in this 'grand old dame'. Consisting of a network of 12 standard rooms, 11 superior rooms and five suites in six private villas, interspersed with serene reflective pools, ponds and colourful gardens, it remains a beguiling paradise despite – or perhaps because of – its slightly faded charm. None of the rooms has a television, a fact that doubtless adds to the rustic appeal, and all are equipped with antique furnishings, impeccably designed bathrooms and minimalist salons which conjure up a feeling of traditional living while ensuring an atmosphere of gentle repose. Villas have their own private gardens and pools, and the classy, discreet service completes the stunning overall ambience. Recently a new bar and salon have been added to maintain the feeling of exclusivity and intimacy.

**Style 10, Atmosphere 9, Location 7**

● **Les Jardins de la Koutoubia, 26 rue de la Koutoubia, Medina.**
Tel: 0 44 38 88 00 www.lesjardinsdelakoutoubia.com
Rates: 2,400–10,000dh

Les Jardins de la Koutoubia stands on the site of the 13th-century Riad Ouarzazi. The owner – a wealthy French textile manufacturer – was merciless in tearing down what was one of the biggest *riads* in town (it held 25 families), and erecting this giant hotel in its place. By five-star hotel standards, it boasts the requisite amount of style and intimacy. The wooden, linear reception leads out into a massive courtyard dominated by a huge pool and verdant gardens. The salons around the pool are a talking-point with their traditional furnishings – immense lamps, jewellery, bookcases – all in Brobdingnagian proportions. The rooms, while pleasant enough and boasting all the expected comforts, haven't been invested with quite the same sense of innovation and charm, though they are sleek and elegant. In addition there are two fine restaurants where you can enjoy an inexpensive lunch (**see** page 85), a wonderful piano bar (see page 115), a jacuzzi on the roof with views over the Koutoubia and a spa, *hammam* and fitness centre.

**Style 7/8, Atmosphere 7, Location 9**

**Les Jardins de la Medina, 21 rue Derb Chtouka, Kasbah, Medina.**
Tel: 0 44 38 18 51 www.lesjardinsdelamedina.com
Rates: 800–1,350dh

Les Jardins de la Medina is pitched somewhere between the personalized setting of a *maison d'hôte* and the less intimate feel of a chain hotel. Located in the Kasbah area of the Medina, it boasts 36 rooms in total and the kind of facilities you'd expect from a large hotel, such as a swimming pool, restaurant, bar, *hammam* and extensive beauty parlour. The rooms are corporate in style (they come with air-conditioning, satellite TV and all the usual mod-cons) though they possess a certain charm with it, which is

enhanced by terraces or balconies. The swimming pool and the gardens downstairs are a principal feature and the restaurant boasts an impressive range of local and international dishes (see page 90). The staff are professional but friendly enough to help ensure your stay here is a relaxed and memorable experience.

**Style 7, Atmosphere 6, Location 7**

### Jnane Tamsna, Douar Abiad, Palmeraie.
Tel: 0 44 32 93 40 www.tamsna.com
Rates: 2,500–4,500dh

Jnane Tamsna is owned by high-profile Marrakech residents Meryanne Loum-Martin (a Senegalese designer) and her husband Gary J. Martin (an American ethno-botanist). It's the third in the 'Tamsna Trilogy' after the restaurant (Riad Tamsna in the Medina: see page100) and the private villa Dar Tamsna (close by to Jnane). It has managed to attract a host of A-list celebrities, including Brad Pitt, David Bowie and Giorgio Armani. The perfect Moorish arches, grandiose drawing room and organic gardens are immediately enchanting, conjuring up an idyllic version of contemporary Moroccan living. The rooms and villas enhance positive initial impressions with superb polyethnic decoration – textiles from Senegal, Berber rugs and Asian silks create alluring geographical themes. There is also clay tennis court at the back, two wonderful pools, and private gardens attached to some of the rooms. Despite

being highly exclusive the atmosphere is surprisingly down-to-earth.

**Style 9, Atmosphere 9, Location 7**

**Kasbah Agafay, Route de Guemassa, 20km.**
Tel: 0 44 36 86 00 www.kasbahagafay.com
Rates: 4,000–5,000dh

Kasbah Agafay is the brainchild of Moroccan entrepreneur Abel Damoussi. It took three years to buy the Kasbah from its previous 36 owners, and the same time again to restore the building to its current glory. There is no doubt that it is one of the most stunning properties in Morocco; sitting on a rise it has spectacular views out over the desert, the fields and out to the High Atlas and Jebel Toubkal, their highest point. Rooms and suites are built around five

main courtyards, connected by a veritable labyrinth of corridors. The décor combines traditional Moroccan with contemporary styles but it's the lavish attention to detail that makes Agafay stand out (Berber tent poles in the four-poster beds; antique keys as lavatory-paper holders). As well as the bedrooms in the Kasbah there are four tented rooms outside whose entire sides open out onto the landscape – incredibly romantic if not particularly intimate. A full set of amenities is on offer, which include a meditation cave, *hamman*, spa centre, floodlit tennis court, large pool, divine drawing room and restaurant. If you don't want to stay here you can come for lunch, to sit by the pool and relax and attend the cookery school, complete with its own kitchen garden.

**Style 9, Atmosphere 10, Location 6**

**Kasbah des Roses, Route de Ouazarzate, Km 9.**
Tel: 0 44 32 93 05 www.kasbahdesroses.com
Rates: 1,300–1,800dh

If you want to be away from it all in a truly intimate environment, the Kasbah des Roses is an astute option. It's only 10 minutes' drive from Marrakech, but that is distance enough from the rumble of the city and the populated Palmeraie area. The place takes its name from the fact that it was – and still is – a functioning rose farm (90% of the produce ends up in Europe, the rest at local markets). The house is located within 15 acres of land, which has not only roses aplenty but also olive groves, bougainvillea and other assorted flora. There are four rooms, all differently designed with themes that swing from Berber to Art Deco and feature some cool modern flourishes in between (check out the funky *zellije*). Three of the rooms back onto a garden, while a smaller one overlooks the large patio furnished with orange and citrus trees. The owners, Lamia and Jawad Berrada, live in the house next door to the main accommodation and make sure all needs, such as meals on site and day trips, are catered for. Quiet, restful and understated this is the perfect place to get away from it all.

**Style 7, Atmosphere 8, Location 7**

**Kasbah du Toubkal, Imlil, Asni, High Atlas.**
Tel: 0 44 48 56 11 www.kasbahdutoubkal.com
Rates: 900–2,500dh

The village of Imlil is the starting-point for the ascension of Mount Toubkal, the highest peak in North Africa. There are plenty of backpackers and hotels in the village but the Kasbah is without a doubt the premier accommodation spot, not just in Imlil but in the whole of the High Atlas region as well. The place is a peaceful, rustic mountain retreat with respectable ecologically friendly policies such as collecting rubbish from local villages, recycling, filtering spring water and generally encouraging responsible tourism. There

is a range of different sleeping arrangements, from dorms and standard rooms to suites, self-catering-style apartments (with kitchen/living room/all mod-cons). Other amenities include a wonderful restaurant (no alcohol is sold on site, but you are free to bring your own), *hammam* and plunge pool, and a panoramic roof terrace that looks out over local villages and verdant valleys. All climbs and treks can be arranged through the Kasbah staff; prices range from 25dh for a half-day trek to 200dh per person for a full ascent, all with guides, cooks, mules, accommodation and drinks (if required). A trip to the Kasbah is a beautiful way to spend a few days away from the hustle and bustle of the city; and a great place to start and end a Toubkal climb or other High Atlas walk.

**Style 8, Atmosphere 9, Location 6**

**Ksar Char-Bagh, Palmeraie de Marrakech, Palmeraie.**
Tel: 0 44 32 92 44 www.ksarcharbagh.com
Rates: 5,500–8,500dh

Marrakech has finally found a hotel to rival the Amanjena in terms of pure luxury and indulgence, but with a little more intimacy. Originally owners Patrick and Nicole Levillair were looking for somewhere in the south of France; unable to find the perfect place, they came to Marrakech to unwind but immediately fell in love with the town, and decided to build somewhere spectacular from scratch. Constructed in the tradition of a Moroccan kasbah, Ksar Char-Bagh is styled as a palace hotel, with 12 *harims*

(rooms), a *hammam*, swimming pool, first-class restaurant and roof terraces with showers and Berber tents. It was an immediate success – the Levillairs have fascinated the exclusive clientele that Ksar Char-Bagh was designed to attract. What makes it so special is the attention to detail – silk *djellabas*, bathrobes and toiletries individually fashioned for men and women, as well as the intricate ornamentation on everything from pillows to ashtrays, all designed by the owners. Here you'll find unparalleled comfort and service, on offer in romantic and select surroundings.

**Style 9/10, Atmosphere 9, Location 7**

**La Maison Arabe, 1 Derb Assehbe, Bab Doukkala, Medina.**
Tel: 0 44 38 70 10 www.lamaisonarabe.com
Rates: 1,500–6,000dh

La Maison Arabe was initially opened 60 years ago as a restaurant by two European ladies and became a popular 'hang-out' for distinguished diplomats and travellers (including Winston Churchill). Having closed in 1983, it was reopened a few years ago as a luxury hotel by an Italian prince. The rooms – 11 standards and two suites – are built around two flower-filled patios and contain a host of modern conveniences, from air-conditioning and telephones to televisions, subtly sitting amid the more traditional décor (some rooms have fireplaces or private terraces). Built using mostly local methods and materials, the hotel has successfully retained some of the nostalgic charm of a bygone era, although

the rooms possess a more corporate aesthetic: think decorative *gebs* and *bejmat* floor-tiling alongside leather desks and minibars. In accordance with the pristine setting, the staff can be overly formal but the facilities – suave Moroccan restaurant, massive pool, cooking school, etc. – far outweigh any negative aspects. The cookery school (500–1600dh depending on the size of the group) and pool are a 10-minute ride away (transport supplied by the hotel) in the Palmeraie, but are exclusively for the use of the guests.

> **Style 8, Atmosphere 8, Location 8**

> **Maison Mnabha, 32–33 Derb Mnabha, Kasbah, Medina.**
> Tel: 0 44 38 13 25 www.maisonmnabha.com
> Rates: 800–1,040dh (closed August)

Maison Mnabha is a curious place operated by English half-brothers Peter Dyer and Lawrence Brady. They have occupied the house for a decade but three years ago decided to open it up to the public as a guesthouse. The biggest attraction is the

reception area, which was part of an old 17th-century palace and boasts original architecture complete with carved wood, calligraphic plasterwork and painted pillars and ceilings. It certainly has a royally refined appeal, although the gloomy ambience downstairs contrasts against the more modern and breezier upstairs area, which contains the four main bedrooms and private and public roof terraces. The rooms are not large, but are modern and comfortable, and with their complementary mix of south-east Asian décor – Buddha heads, silks from Laos – and Moroccan ornamentation, are good value for money. The main terrace has great views over the Kasbah, Les Jardins Agdal and the Bahia Palace. Peter rather handily has a PhD on the Kasbah and is a fountain of local knowledge. Snacks and dinner are made to order and a digital television offers programmes in English. The only drawback is that it is a little out of the way with a 15-minute walk through the Medina to the Jemaa el Fna.

**Style 7, Atmosphere 7, Location 8**

**La Mamounia, Avenue Bab Jedid, Medina.**
Tel: 0 44 44 44 09 www.mamounia.com
Rates: 2,850–30,000dh

There's not much to say about the legendary Mamounia hotel that hasn't already been said – apart from saying that much of what has been said is true. Yes, it's the most well known and most opulent location in all of Marrakech. Yes, it has put up a host of world-famous guests ranging from the Prince of Wales to Mick Jagger. And, yes, these days it lives largely on its past glory rather than any ongoing sense of wonder and achievement. Architects Prost and Marchisio, who fused Moroccan architecture with the predominant art-deco style of the era, built the place in 1922. It was renovated in 1986 but the fusion remains

intact, making for an old-fashioned and elegant hotel that still gives off airs of refinement and luxury to the 'right' people – and of unnecessary haughtiness to the 'wrong' ones. There are 171 rooms, 57 suites and three separate, exclusive villas, which are all as comfortable and thoroughly equipped as you might expect. As well as the sleeping quarters, there is a whole other Mamounia-world to explore, complete with amusement arcades, gardens, casino, several bars, swimming pool, jacuzzis, tennis and squash courts, gym, sauna, beauty service, boutiques and five restaurants.

**Style 7, Atmosphere 6, Location 8**

**Riad Bab Firdaus, 57–58 rue Bahia, Medina.**
Tel: 0 44 38 00 73 www.babfirdaus.com
Rates: 1,600–3,500dh

Bab Firdaus ('Gateway To Heaven') is one of the newest spots in town, opened at the end of 2003. Styled as a dual-purpose *riad* and restaurant, it boasts a small but cute Mediterranean restaurant just off the elegant main courtyard and a Berber grill up on the mud-walled terrace. The seven rooms have king-sized beds and 24-hour room service. They are all different sizes, with one or two of the smaller ones being perhaps a little too cosy, while the suites contain more than enough space. The overriding theme throughout is Berber-inspired, with soft colour themes, chests, pictures, saddles, rugs adorning the floors and walls, and

bathrooms done out in *tadelakt*. There is also a traditional *hammam* and solarium. A Berber tent on the roof is a great place to lie back with a mint tea and do some stargazing.

**Style 7, Atmosphere 7, Location 8**

**Riad El Cadi, 87 Derb Moulay Abdelkader, Dabachi, Medina.**
Tel: 0 44 37 86 55 www.riyadelcadi.com
Rates: 1,100–2,650dh

Part *maison d'hôte*, part museum, El Cadi is famous for its stunning collection of rare antiquities and textiles, the personal property of late owner Herwig Bartels (a former German ambassador). The building dates back to the 13th and 14th centuries, which makes it much older than many. The winding staircases and twisting corridors are made up of five interconnected houses with patios, all of which still bear separate names and identities and can be rented out in their entirety. The four ground-floor rooms have en-suite showers while the eight first-floor rooms all have bathrooms. The impeccably tasteful decoration (ancient Berber costumes, antique textiles from the Atlas, Ottoman embroideries) that is spread throughout the public areas extends to the rooms. There's a separate gallery space for a more formal textile display. Add highly discreet and superbly efficient service and a range of in-house facilities (swimming pool, jacuzzi, *hammam*, well-equipped library, large terraces, dining and conference rooms) and you have a uniquely refined,

private and remarkable atmosphere that you won't want to leave in a hurry.

**Style 9, Atmosphere 9, Location 8**

**Riad El Fenn, 2 Derb Moulay Abdallah Ben Hezzian, Bab El Ksour, Medina.**
Tel: 0 44 44 12 10  www.riadelfenn.com
Rates: 2,900–4,400dh

Due to open its doors fully to the public in October 2004, Vanessa Branson's ultra-chic *riad* is set to become the most talked-about *maison d'hôte* in Marrakech for some time to come. Situated at the edge of the Medina, 5 minutes' walk from the Jemaa el Fna, Riad El Fenn has been designed as a family home, an artistic retreat and a commercial business. The six suites and three rooms are arranged around an elegant courtyard, while elsewhere in the building there are two swimming pools, a massage and *hammam* centre, a home cinema and a kitchen for cooking lessons, as well as wi-fi internet connection. The style of the house is unique: simple *tadelakt* rooms are painted in turquoise blues, deep reds and simple creams; and with decorations that vary from Murano chandeliers picked up in the Portobello Road to works by acclaimed international artists such as Bridget Riley, Terry Frost and Fiona Rae, it hopes to communicate a creative and stimulating ambience. Comfort is of the essence, and a great deal of emphasis has been put on service,

which is provided by consummate hosts/managers Frederic Scholl and Viviana Gonzalez.

**Style 9, Atmosphere 9, Location 9**

**Riad El Jazira, 7–8 Derb Mayara, Sidi Ben Slimane, Medina.**
Tel: 0 44 42 64 63 www.marrakech-riads.net
Rates: 800dh

El Jazira is one of the newer acquisitions for the prolific Marrakech Riads (who also own, for example, Dar Zellije, Dar Sara, Dar Baraka and the Café Literaire – see pages 39 and 127). Made up of three adjoining houses, it is one of the biggest houses in the Medina, containing no fewer than 15 rooms. The buildings have been refurbished so that they are all quite different from each other. One is a modern, 20th-century-style property painted in restrained vanillas and coffees with minimalist décor; another is overtly 18th-century with original features meeting some modest restoration work, and is peppered with straw *hassira* carpets (the kind found in mosques), hike curtains and simple Berber rugs. A third house is decidedly the most opulent of the lot, particularly the courtyard with its exquisite emerald pool, white alcoves and raised platform area. The rooms vary from charming to ascetic but the overall feeling is one of authenticity.

**Style 7, Atmosphere 8, Location 7**

**Riad El Mezouar, 28 Derb El Hamman, Issebtinne, Medina.**
Tel: 0 44 38 09 49 www.mezouar.com
Rates: 1,700–1,950dh

Located near the Ben Youssef Medersa, the delightful and stylish El Mezouar is the creation of young French designers Jerome Vermelin and Michel Durand-Meyrier. It used to be an 18th-century palace, 'Mezouar' being the official title bestowed upon the branch of the Alaoui royal family who used to own it. The present owners have worked hard to maintain something of its original feel, especially around the courtyard, which has a tradi-tional-style pool and Arabo–Andalucian arcades and galleries. There are five rooms, which emphasize the natural spaces and contours of the building; rather than cramming them full of fea-tures, they have settled on a policy of quality and taste over quantity. Their own designs feature here and there among imported Chinese, Byzantine and Tibetan ornamentation. Food (French and Moroccan) is available on the premises, made by an excellent local chef, and can be taken in the Moorish alcoves, the grand salons, the courtyard or the terrace.

**Style 8, Atmosphere 7, Location 8**

**Riad Enija, 9 Derb Mesfioui, Rahba Lakdima, Medina.**
Tel: 0 44 44 09 26 www.riadenija.com
Rates: 2,350–3,500dh (closed July)

Swedish architect Bjorn Conerdings and Swiss designer Ursula Haldimann have transformed this 200-year-old silk-traders' townhouse (around a third of it is still intact) into a living, breathing work of art. The pair collect far-out contemporary pieces, and love to juxtapose their personal mementos against more traditional decorative touches. Hence the 12 suites – which have names such as 'Lion', 'Chameleon' and 'Prince' – are kitted out with sculpted wrought-iron four-poster beds, silk floor cushions, Chantille Saccmanno tables and Alan Girell/Mark Brazer mirrors. It can all be a little too much at times, but mostly it conspires to create a charmingly eccentric and discernibly unique atmosphere. Other attractions include a terrace, a leafy courtyard, a small pool on the roof, a beauty parlour, a Moroccan kitchen and a large public salon – all of which are maintained by a veritable army of girls (27 to be exact) who float around in elegant red outfits.

**Style 9, Atmosphere 8, Location 8**

**Riad Farnatchi, 2 Derb Farnatchi, Qua'at Benahid.**
Tel: 0 44 38 49 10  www.riadfarnatchi.com
Rates: 2,950–4,400dh

This exquisitely decorated *riad* opened in March 2004. Originally

designed as the home of Jonathan Wix, the man behind The
Scotsman in Edinburgh and Hotel de la Tremoille in Paris,
Farnatchi has instantly become part of Marrakech's elite accommodation. The renovation took two years to complete, culminat-
ing in a stylish fusion of modern European and traditional

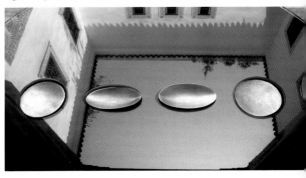

Marrakchi design. Designed around two courtyards, the five
suites are simple and elegant, affording guests the requisite intimacy as well as the comfort associated with Jonathan's other
hotels. Tucked away in the narrow alleyways north of the souks,
Farnatchi is not the easiest *riad* to find, and don't even think
about trying to reach it by car – it is surrounded by small artisans' workshops and a bustling local community. Its real selling-
point is Lynn, the manageress, whose superb knowledge of
Marrakech, coupled with her ability to understand the needs of
the guests and advise them on how best to spend their time, is
worth a fortune alone.

**Style 9, Atmosphere 8, Location 9**

**Riad Ifoulki, 11 Derb Moqqadem, Arset Loghzail, Medina.**
Tel: 0 44 38 56 56 www.riadifoulki.com
Rates: 1,500–3,000dh

Ifoulki's main attraction lies in its continued resistance to the
'designer *riad*' boom that has assailed Marrakech since the late
1990s. While many have been busy transforming their locales into
*Vogue*-esque visions of contemporary cool, Dutch owner Peter

Bergmann and son have kept Ifoulki's atmosphere distinctly traditional. This means that the space, which is made up several royal houses, has a fairly austere quality, but the advantage is of course

a much bigger sense of authenticity, not to mention larger rooms. The main courtyard especially – a grand old place full of jasmine, olive and orange trees – has impressively big dimensions, while the rooms that run around it are correspondingly large. The place carries a sophisticated and discreet air, enhanced by the presence of the Bergmanns (who speak 10 languages between them) and by touches like a well-stocked multilingual library, music and culture evenings (which include 'courses' on everything from psychology to Sufi mysticism), a broad selection of fine antiques and an atmosphere of refined congeniality. Its broad appeal extends to holidaying families, celebrities and foreign diplomats alike.

**Style 7, Atmosphere 8, Location 8**

**Riad Kaiss, 65 Derb Jedid (off Riad Zitoune El Kedim), Medina.**
Tel: 0 44 44 01 41 www.riadkaiss.com
Rates: 1,465–2,260dh

It took three years to transform Kaiss from a local *riad* (dating from 1860) into the fine guesthouse it is now. Owned and constructed by architect Christian Ferre (who still lives here) it's a sizeable place centred around two large courtyards, which, along with the rooms, are littered with a considered amalgam of antiques, art-deco furnishings, objects from Thailand and a plethora of neatly arranged artistic bits and bobs. The eight rooms all differ décor-wise but are unerring in their quest to seduce romantic souls. The roof is really something to behold: a handsome, florid network of stairways and relaxation areas with a natty plunge pool tucked away discreetly in one corner. The staff can be aloof but the level of service seems more than decent. Other facilities include a fitness room, *hammam* and meals cooked to order on the premises.

**Style 7, Atmosphere 7, Location 8**

**Riad Mabrouka, 56 Derb El Bahia (off Riad Zitoun El Jedid), Medina.**
Tel: 0 44 37 75 79 www.riad-mabrouka.com
Rates: 1,400–1,800dh

Riad Mabrouka is named after Mabrouka Bent Salem Bouida, the grandmother of owner Catherine Neri, who opened this place as a tribute. Those who like the idea of balancing Zen-styled interiors with funky minimalist furnishings should not hesitate to seek it out. Built by architect Christophe Simeon, it's a cool but elegant rush of harmony and tastefully restrained artfulness. Wooden furnishings, white walls, a beautiful courtyard with a trickling show-pool, antique packing trunks and *tadelakt* bathrooms are balanced against a seductive savannah backdrop of greys, whites and browns, all repeated in strategically placed giant mirrors. The two suites and three double rooms are similarly delightful, though they walk the tightrope between cosy and small. There are salons downstairs for relaxing in, a lovely roof terrace and traditional Moroccan food is available on order. The Musée de Marrakech is nearby.

**Style 8/9, Atmosphere 8, Location 8**

**Riad Mehdi, 2 Derb Sedra, Bab Agnaou, Medina.**
Tel: 0 44 38 47 13 www.riadmehdi.com
Rates: 1,000–2,600dh

With five suites (including a duplex apartment-style chamber) and four standard double rooms, an extensive spa and *hammam* complex next door, plus a good location just inside the Bab Agnaou gate, Riad Mehdi is an all-round attractive proposition. The usual runs of smooth *tadelakt* walls, *zellije* tiling and *bejmat* floors are found throughout the place, although since it was built from scratch three years ago, a certain feeling of modernity creeps through the décor. Rooms aren't as large as they could be but they are certainly adequate, and decorated unostentatiously with comfort and sensuality rather than hipness in mind. The outside courtyard backs onto the ancient medina walls. It's a

divine little hideaway with a regulated temperature pool, a bar just inside the main doors and even a small dining area. If you want a holiday packed with relaxation, health and beauty then this could well be the right place for you. (See page 182.)

**Style 7, Atmosphere 7, Location 8**

**Riad Noga, 78 Derb Jdid, Douar Graoua, Medina.**
Tel: 0 44 37 76 70 www.riadnoga.com
Rates: 1,430–2,090dh

Entering Riad Noga you are met by an otherworld of vivid yellows and bold pinks which contrast against a tree-lined main courtyard with inviting green-tiled swimming pool and suave relaxation areas. Through a Moorish arch is another house with a more traditionally decorated courtyard, full of orange trees and bougainvillea, with intimate spaces, divans and Berber cushions encouraging supine activities. The Riad's seven rooms are all dressed in different colours, with traditional themes enhanced by the vaulted ceilings, handcrafted wooden doors, original paintings and *tadelakt* bathrooms. Despite the local influences the colours and mod-cons make the rooms feel quite contemporary. They're modestly sized, though some have private roof terraces where meals can be taken in isolation. More sociable types can head downstairs and dine in a pleasant salon custom-built for groups.

**Riad 72, 72 Arset Awzel, Bab Doukkala, Medina.**
Tel: 0 44 38 76 29 www.riad72.com
Rates: 900–2,500dh

Riad 72 is small but perfectly formed, constructed around an
ultra-relaxing courtyard. The owner, a Milanese photographer
named Giovanna, has a great sense of style that puts an Italian
twist on traditional Moroccan décor to create a cool, funky and
luxurious environment. The four rooms vary in size dramatically
and contain artistically designed beds but all have gorgeous bathrooms with basins made from barrels and beaten copper, and differently coloured *tadelakt* walls. The main suite is the largest

room and has the bonus of a wonderful built-in sunlight. This makes the room next door seem small, although in actual fact it is a perfectly reasonable size and has an en-suite bathroom to die for (and at half the price of the bigger room, it is well worth the money). Riad 72 is slightly taller than most, affording great views from the attractively attired roof terrace, and the service and ambience are superbly intimate.

**Style 8, Atmosphere 8, Location 8**

**Sherazade, 3 Derb Djama (off Riad Zitoun El Kedim), Medina.**
Tel: 0 44 42 93 05 sharezade@iam.net.ma
Rates: 150–600dh

The Sherazade has for a long time been one of the premier picks for the budget fraternity, and it's not hard to see why. The hotel consists of two large connected courtyards, with 19 bed-

rooms positioned around them. Visitors are greeted with bub-bling fountains and colourful tiling. Rooms are small and basic but clean and comfortable with the patios and a roof terrace providing extra space. The terrace is in fact especially pleasant, with views, abundant foliage, iron tables and chairs and even a traditional cushioned tent in which you can take meals. The own-ers and staff are friendly, multilingual, and happy to give advice and arrange day trips. Definitely good value for money, which is why you should book ahead to reserve a room. As a curious aside, there is a range of traditional Moroccan and Pakistani clothing on sale in the foyer.

> **Style 6, Atmosphere 8, Location 8**

**La Sultana, Rue de la Kasbah, Kasbah, Medina.**
Tel: 0 44 38 80 08 www.lasultanamarakech.com
Rates: 2,000–7,680dh

La Sultana finally opened its doors to the public in the spring of 2004, immediately becoming the Leading Hotels of the World's choice in Marrakech. Located just off a busy drag and overlooking the historically important Saadian Tombs, the Sultana is a meticulously renovated palace, which took two years and required experienced local craftsmen to reconstruct the classical Moroccan architecture. The 21 rooms are ranged over three levels and around four separate courtyards, and unlike many of the *riad* hotels in the Medina La Sultana offers an impressive array of traditional and modern extras – from *objets d'art* to DVD players. An impressive roof terrace is sympathetically designed so as not to detract from the neighbouring monument, but does incorporate an open-air massage centre and a quiet space for sun-downer drinks; a swimming pool set in a verdant courtyard helps to ease the heat of the day.

> **Style 8, Atmosphere 8, Location 8**

**Tchaikana, 25 Derb El Ferrane, Kaat Benahid, Medina.**
Tel: 0 44 38 51 50 www.tchaikana.com
Rates: 800–1,500dh

Run by ultra-hospitable Belgian couple Delphine and Jean-Francois, Tchaikana is simply one of the best value-for-money *riads* in the Medina. Delphine used to jaunt around Africa looking for artefacts and crafts to trade in the art store she had in Brussels before moving here. Now her collection creates a tasteful Sub-Saharan theme throughout this slickly minimalist haven of tranquillity. Wall hangings, furnishings and ornamentation are

strewn carefully across a backdrop of restrained browns and beiges in rooms as big as suites, and suites that could double as aircraft hangars. The bathrooms are features in their own right, voluptuous and rustic with beautiful touches such as beaten-copper basins. Downstairs, much of the original 19th-century design has been kept intact (stucco detailing, cedarwood doors), and surrounds a romantic courtyard overlooked by orange and citrus trees and enclosed by rooms and salons. The owners are relaxed, hip and very knowledgeable about local culture, making this a great option for style-conscious travellers.

**Style 8, Atmosphere 9, Location 8**

**Tichka Salam, Route de Casablanca, Semlalia.**
Tel: 0 44 44 87 10 www.groupesalam.com
Rates: 1,200–3,300dh

The Tichka – known affectionately as the 'Little Mamounia' – is a bit of an institution in Marrakech. In fact, it feels a tad institutional, too, since the days when it was looked on as an ultra-sleek designer hotspot for the stars (it was designed by American architectural legend Bill Willis) are long gone, and it has now acquired a reputation as a slightly faded corporate hotel. Significantly, however, there is still evidence of what made it a talking-point in the first place, such as the kitsch palm-tree pillars in the restaurant, the funky swimming pool, the eye-catching room furnishings. The upkeep has been slack and a sense of formal austerity dampens the sense of fun somewhat, but there are plenty of conveniences (a new business suite and fitness centre, and all 138 rooms have TVs and minibars) and it's still slightly ahead of other big-scale hotels in the charm stakes. If you're going to go big, you might as well go Tichka.

**Style 6, Atmosphere 7, Location 7**

**Tigmi, Route d'Amizmiz, Douar Tagadert, Ait el kadi Tamslouht.**
Tel: 0 66 93 49 64 www.tigmi.com
Rates: 1,500–5,000dh

Tigmi is co-owned by the same people who represent Caravanserei but, instead of being in an Arabic village, this place is in a Berber village ('tigmi' means 'house' in Berber). The village

in question is located at a high altitude overlooking a verdant and very picturesque valley, complete with river and hills. Boccara's distinctive touch is again evident, his subtle dreamtime architecture infused with an incredible sense of calm and rustic mystique. The eight suites are all showpieces in themselves, managing to combine the vividly exotic with an otherworldly charm. They all have separate bedrooms, sitting rooms and bathrooms and most have fireplaces for the winter evening chill. Amenities include a secluded TV room, a pool right near the external wall that overlooks the village and plenty of surprise alcoves and arches. In fact, it may well be a cut above Caravanserei because of its fantastic situation and slightly more Arcadian appeal.

**Style 9, Atmosphere 10, Location 6**

**Topkapi, Tamsna, Route de Fes, Km 4, Palmaraie.**
Tel: 0 44 32 98 89 www.topkapi-marrakech.com
Rates: 1,500–1,700dh

Charming French couple Dmitri and Letitiae (the daughter of fashion designer Madame Baconnier) have created something quite special with Topkapi. Located not far along Route de

Fes in the Palmeraie, it has a different feel from most other places, courtesy of a design by a local architect and the down-to-earth homely atmosphere cultivated by the owners. Walk through the big anonymous double doors to find two elegant and striking buildings. One houses the reception area, an appealing bar, relaxation salon and dining rooms that lead out to an outdoor pool. Behind this are 10 rooms, arranged around a two-tier Spanish-style *riad*. They're all similarly designed in pretty and refined fashion. The lower rooms adjoin the gardens while the upstairs ones have walk-in bathrooms leading off the main bedroom and better access to the roof terrace (from where the sunset is spectacular). There's also a wonderful 'old style' *hammam* to relax in, with *gommage* scrub-downs and massages on offer.

Style 8, Atmosphere 8, Location 7

**Villa Des Orangers, 6 rue Sidi Mimoun, Place Ben Tachfine, Medina.**
Tel: 0 44 38 46 38 www.villadesorangers.com
Rates: 2,900–6,000dh

Blink and you'll miss the unassuming entrance to the only Relais & Chateaux member in Morocco. Right on the bustling Rue Sidi Mimoun, close to the Jemaa El Fna, and overlooking a decidedly unglamorous petrol station (as well as the Koutoubia Mosque), its location is unlikely yet convenient for one of the most highly

regarded accommodation spots in town. Once inside the doors, the heat and sweat of the outside world drifts away and your senses feast instead on the water channels full of floating rose petals, orange-treed courtyard, alcoves full of soft sofas and the gently gurgling fountains. The 19 rooms and suites are all spacious – stylish, but with a sense of patient sophistication – and the atmosphere is generally low-key, making it a major draw for well-to-do Europeans and the odd celebrity. The recent opening of a new courtyard means there is now a good size pool on the ground floor as well as on the roof terrace, a massage centre, boutique and three brand new suites. Although this has improved the facilities it has lost a little of the intimacy so associated with Marrakech's *riads*.

**Style 9, Atmosphere 9, Location 9**

# eat...

Eating in Marrakech is a surprisingly diverse and delightful experience. The last few years have seen a rise in chic, internationally focused restaurants – mainly French and Italian – that compete with the more traditional Moroccan hotspots and make for a varied selection of options.

The prices and quality of the food vary, of course. You can pick up a bite on street stalls such as those on the Jemaa El Fna for under 50dh, or pay considerably more to eat somewhere more exclusive, although even then you rarely pay more than 600dh.

For one of the more filling culinary adventures on offer, head for what is known colloquially as a 'palace' restaurant. These places – so-called because they are often housed in old 18th- or 19th-century palace buildings – fulfil every fantasy of what a traditional Moroccan dining experience should be: classic Moroccan décor, waiters in traditional outfits, bubbling fountains, tables strewn with rose petals, exotic (belly) dancers and so much tasty food it borders on torture since there is no way you can fit it all in.

Pay your fixed fee and the routine begins, usually with a platter of *hors d'oeuvres* (*briouettes*: deep fried envelopes of filo pastry containing anything from ground

meat to cheese), followed by a starter (*pastilla*: a larger and sweeter wrap of filo pastry containing chicken or pigeon, cooked with almonds, spices, cinnamon and sugar), a couple of main courses (a *tajine*: a stew of meat and/or vegetables cooked with spices and fruit and served in conical dishes; and couscous: ground semolina flour served with meat and/or vegetables), then anything between one and three different desserts.

It's a memorable way to sample the local cuisine – one experience is usually more than enough. If your stomach is a little more human-sized you might want to dine à la carte. Bear in mind that Moroccans usually serve *tajines* and couscous at home (the latter is often eaten from a large shared pot with the right hand), so these dishes are the most commonplace in restaurants to the point where they can quickly become underwhelming or even uninviting. *Mechoui* (lamb slowly roasted in a great outdoor oven pit) is a local dish well worth looking out for.

As a general rule, the more modern restaurants are located in Gueliz while the more traditional spots are in the Medina, although there are exceptions, of course, such as Riad Tamsna, Le Foundouk, Tobsil, Le Pavillon and Dar Moha – which are all chic places hidden among the old city's narrow alleyways.

The prices quoted here represent the average cost of a starter and main course for one person, with a glass of wine.

**Our top ten restaurants in Marrakech are:**
1. Dar Moha
2. Le Tobsil
3. La Trattoria di Giancarlo
4. Ksar Char-Bagh
5. L'Italien
6. Le Foundouk
7. Riad Tamsna
8. Dar Marjana
9. Jad Mahal
10. Al Fassia

**The top five for food are:**
1. Dar Moha
2. La Trattoria di Giancarlo
3. Le Tobsil
4. Ksar Char-Bagh
5. Al Fassia

**The top five for service are:**
1. La Trattoria di Giancarlo
2. Dar Moha
3. Riad Tamsna
4. Le Tobsil
5. Ksar Char-Bagh

**The top five for atmosphere are:**
1. Jemaa El Fna
2. Le Foundouk
3. Le Tobsil
4. Jad Mahal
5. Riad Tamsna

**Al Baraka, I Place Jemaa El Fna, Medina.**
Tel: 0 44 44 23 41 www.albaraka.to
Open: noon–3pm, 8–10.30pm daily                    475dh

Heralded by a large sign in the corner of the square, Al Baraka
used to be the home of a Marrakech pacha. A large, white-tile
*riad* with an enormous tree-filled courtyard and ostentatiously
decorated alcoves and dining rooms, it gives you some idea of
the luxurious lifestyle of Morocco's 18th- and 19th-century
ruling classes. The outside seats around 25 people with inner
alcoves providing space for another 35 or so. There are a few
set-menu options here, which range from the 300dh 'Menu du

Caid' to the 400dh 'Menu du Calife'. They all feature the usual
run of *tajines*, *pastillas*, salads and couscous in varying combina-
tions and flavours. In the evenings belly-dancers undulate to
Andalucian music and the whole thing can be extremely amusing.
The only potential problem is that the place is popular with tour
groups; if you're keen to avoid these it's best to book ahead and
ask. Ideally placed for an after dinner wander around the Jemaa
El Fna to check out the story tellers and the henna artists.

| Food 7, Service 8, Atmosphere 7 |

**Al Fassia, 232 Avenue Mohammed V, Gueliz.**
Tel: 0 44 43 40 60 alfassia@iam.net.ma
Open: noon–2.30pm, 7.30–11pm daily                    250dh

Owned and run solely by women, Al Fassia is a unique proposition in Morocco. A traditional and elegant space, it is well tended by the owners, who busy themselves efficaciously, with sleeves rolled up, around large circular tables, creating an atmosphere of attentive relaxation. Large traditional paintings

adorn the walls, the silk napkins have been studiously embroidered, and the overall impression is of eating in some-one's (opulent) home. The menu is as traditional as the interior, and has à la carte or fixed menu options. All the classic dishes make an appearance and there are a few more innovative ones. Frustration kicks in at the specials page: they look incredible but must be ordered 24 hours in advance. Fortunately the regular menu provides some of the best local cuisine in town and, with wines and beers now available, you might not want to restrict your time here.

**Food 9, Service 8, Atmosphere 7**

**Alizia, On the corner of Chouhada and Rue Ahmed Chawki, Gueliz/Hivernage.**
Tel: 0 44 43 83 60
Open: noon–3pm, 7–11.30pm daily                    250dh

Alizia is an intimate little Italian in the Gueliz/Hivernage area (not far from Le Comptoir), run by the incredibly amiable Miss Rachida. The main gates lead into a lovely garden courtyard, with

bougainvillea and other assorted foliage held back from the tables by wooden fencing. There's a decidedly romantic atmosphere here and it is obviously the prime dining spot. Inside is a tiny, two-tiered space, which is also very intimate and homely. The menu has an elaborate mix of tasty pastas and great pizzas, but also features more substantial Italian-style fish and meat dishes too. The constant presence of Miss Rachida ensures everything runs very smoothly and is doubtless why it enjoys plenty of repeat custom.

**Food 8, Service 8, Atmosphere 8**

**L'Amandier, On the corner of the Rue de Paris and Avenue Echouhada, Gueliz/Hivernage.**
Tel: 0 44 44 60 93 www.lamandier.com
Open: 11–2.30pm, 6pm–midnight daily                    300dh

'Interesting' is the first word that springs to mind when visiting L'Amandier. Hidden from view by a scruffy pink curve of wall bearing its name in flowery lettering, the venue itself is a curious mélange of purple walls, large mirrors, green tablecloths, kitsch paintings and an extra-colourful bar. There's something immediately pleasing about it, and one's sense of satisfaction is deepened by the extensive list of classic French dishes, which are cooked to a high standard and set at a reasonable price. Additional seating is provided in a similar room out the back, and there's a Berber-style tent and extra bar in the garden if the weather's good. The staff aren't the most attentive in the world, but that's in keeping with the relaxed feeling of the place.

**Food 8, Service 7, Atmosphere 7**

### La Bagatelle, 101 Rue Yougoslavie, Gueliz.
Tel: 0 44 43 02 74 bagatelle@menara.ma
Open: noon–2.30pm, 7.30–10.30pm. Closed Wednesday.    230dh

La Bagatelle is a well-established French-run restaurant located in the centre of Gueliz. It's been in the same family since 1949, the current owner being the daughter-in-law of the original patron, while her son now manages the restaurant. The main, vine-covered doors lead directly off the street and into two areas. In all but the coldest weather, people head for the attractive outdoor terrace, where grapes dangle through wooden

trelliswork above your head and foliage rests reassuringly around you. The tried-and-tested menu isn't particularly extensive, but the food – which consists mainly of French-style meat and fish dishes with the odd traditional dish thrown in for good measure – is consistently good, and the staff are relaxed and reliably efficient. For colder weather, there's an indoor section next door with a fireplace to banish the winter chill.

**Food 8, Service 8, Atmosphere 7**

**Bô-Zin, Douar Lohna, Route de l'Ourika, 3.5km.**
Tel: 0 44 38 80 12  www.bo-zin.com
Open: 8pm–1am daily.                                    300dh

Whatever word-play is intended on the name, this place – 3.5km outside of town is a breath of fresh air, with an international menu and an atmosphere that is conducive to kicking off your shoes and leaping onto the tables. The project of three entrepreneurs, one of whom worked at Le Comptoir for many years, has resulted in the creation of one of the most hip restaurants to hit Marrakech in the last three years. Here, as with Jad Mahal, the emphasis is on atmosphere – an intimate but laid-back interior and a beautiful terrace overlooking the Moroccan garden, with music growing gradually louder as the evening wears on, ensure a great night out. The service is attentive but the quality of the food does impinge upon the enjoyment of the whole – while perfectly good, it fails to attain the standard that the restaurant really needs. After only three months of opening, however, it is a problem that should soon be ironed out.

Food 7, Service 8/9, Atmosphere 9

**Catanzaro, 42 Rue Tarek Ibn Ziad, Gueliz.**
Tel: 0 44 43 37 31
Open: noon–2.30pm and 7.30–11pm. Closed Sunday.          150dh

Catanzaro competes with Pizzeria Niagara as the most popular Italian in town. Both of them serve excellent food in homely, down-to-earth environments, but they are presented very differently. Catanzaro surely has the edge in terms of rustic charm, its Artex-ed walls and red-and-white-checked tablecloths (which match the red and white uniforms of the staff) giving the place an unpretentious but lively feel. The food, mostly Italian staples such

as pizza and pasta plus a selection of good grills and fish meals, is delicious. The service is beautifully old-fashioned in the sense that the owners (Genevieve and Jawad) meet and greet everyone on arrival each night and take your payments at the till at the end. The fact that normally housebound Moroccans even come and eat here is testament enough to its charm and quality.

**Food 8, Service 9, Atmosphere 8**

**Les Cepages, 9 Rue Ibn Zaidoun, Gueliz.**
Tel: 0 44 43 94 26 www.ilovemarrakesh.com/lescepages
Open: noon–2pm, 8–11.30pm. Closed Monday.                    310dh

Conveniently located around the corner from the Montecristo bar, Les Cepages has been about for some time, changing its name a while ago to 'Pretexte' but then swiftly changing back again. Located in an elegant villa, it has large, pristine tables

dressed with yellow cloths and white napkins. The traditional décor (ornate mirrors, vases, busts) and a sophisticated ambience seem to suit the wealthier types who frequent it. The menu contains a host of classic French dishes: there aren't too many surprises but what it does, it does very well. The food, although delicious, might be a little too rich for some, but the service is infallible. Les Cepages requires a more formal approach to dress than some of its peers, but it can be relaxed and charming on the right night.

**Food 8, Service 9, Atmosphere 7**

### Chez Chegrouni, Place Jemaa El Fna.

Tel: 0 44 44 53 50

Open: 7am–11pm daily                                         60dh

Chegrouni is no design showroom by any means but it is convenient, and an institution on the Jemaa El Fna. The gated exterior leads through an outdoor terrace to a scruffy, austere room. The green tablecloths, orange bench-seating and *zellije*-covered walls are punctuated with the obligatory pictures of the monarchy. However, what the place lacks in glamour and panache, it makes up for with lots of local character, cheap food and pretty rapid service. The well-thumbed plastic menus offer a predictable range of Moroccan staples such as salads, *tajines*, *harira* soup, omelettes, couscous and grills. When you sit down you'll see a glass full of what appear to be paper napkins, but which are in fact order slips. Jot down what you want and pass it to a speeding waiter, who will return it at the end as your bill-cum-napkin. It's a great place to observe the general bustle of the square among a few of the locals.

Food 6, Service 8, Atmosphere 7

### Le Comptoir, Avenue Rechouada, Gueliz/Hivernage.

Tel: 0 44 43 77 02

Open: 4pm–1am (2.30am Friday and Saturday) daily          425dh

The sister-restaurant of the Parisian Comptoir is THE trendy spot to eat in Marrakech. Dining here will put you amid a veritable list of who's who – or at least those who'd like to be a who. The culinary action takes place in a dark, seductive main room whose suggestive curves and luxurious reds and blacks are reminiscent of a chic Far Eastern opium den. Pretty waitresses

float around in pink designer dresses, musicians massage your ears, and candles illuminate the faces of the local cognoscenti. The menu is predictably unpredictable and perhaps a little ambitious since the standard of the food seems secondary to the experience of actually being there. That said, it's all very good calibre and incredibly tasty (especially the *mechoui*). After the belly-dancers have whirled around a few times, follow the sumptuous stairwell up to the bar area or sashay outdoors to the garden and enjoy a cocktail while reclining against a silky cushion.

**Food 8, Service 8, Atmosphere 9**

**Dar Marjana, 15 Derb Sidi Ali Tair, Bab Doukkala, Medina.**
Tel: 0 44 38 51 10/57 73 www.dar-marjana.com
Open: 8–11pm. Closed Tuesday.                                    700dh

Dar Marjana, a family home for almost one hundred years, was opened to the public as a restaurant 23 years ago. The current patron was born here, and the rest of the family still live on site, though the place feels more like a luxurious palace than a home.

Guests are led into an exquisite cypress-treed courtyard for an aperitif to be sipped on divans among softly glowing lanterns around the central fountain. At serving time, you are then seated in one of the four salons (arranged on two floors) or the roof terrace, whereupon a deluge of delicious food served on plates the size of dustbin lids and in *tajines* the size of small circus tents begins to appear. Quality as well as quantity is evidently the motto here since the food is of an incomparable standard. The atmosphere becomes generally more convivial as the night goes on. By the time your stomach is at bursting-point

and your mind well oiled with fine wine (the fixed price includes unlimited drinks), the music gets louder and a dancer enters the fray, encouraging group participation – a few well-placed notes tucked into her costume are welcome. An unforgettable experience. Reservations are essential.

**Food 9, Service 9, Atmosphere 10**

● **Dar Moha, 81 Rue Dar El Bacha, Medina.**
Tel: 0 44 38 64 00 www.darmoha.ma
Open: noon–3pm, 7.30pm–late. Closed Monday.          400dh

Moha is named after its owner Mohammed, an extrovert Moroccan chef who lived and worked in Switzerland for 14 years before returning and opening this rather fine restaurant. The venue itself used to be a royal *riad* (the palace is just across the road), before Moha transformed it into an ultra-romantic establishment that is considered by many to be the premier dining spot in town. It's difficult to argue. A splendid petal-covered courtyard leads into a spacious room full of large white tables, decorated in refined Moroccan style, with an upstairs that's designed for either group or intimate dining. The best spot, however, is out the back, especially in the evenings, where tables surround a gorgeously luminescent pool and create a beautifully romantic ambience. The cuisine here – traditional Moroccan with a Moha twist – is flawlessly fantastic.

Great care has been taken to ensure the food is devoid of unnecessary fat and sugar but still tastes deliciously satisfying. It's available as à la carte or fixed menu at lunchtimes as well as dinners.

**Food 9, Service 10, Atmosphere 9**

**El Marrakchi, 52 Rue des Banques, Jemaa El Fna, Medina.**
Tel: 0 44 44 33 77 www.lemarrakchi.com
Open 11.30am–11pm daily                                          260dh

El Marrakchi is located opposite the Café de France, and is accessed via dark, incensed stairs that are located to the side of the restaurant, between two buildings. The stairs lead up to two separate floors. The top one is the most popular and has superior views across the square, even though there is no roof terrace; the seating is arranged inwardly, so the views are restricted to pretty much standing up and gazing out of windows. In any case, the ambience on both floors is certainly superior to the other restaurants on the square: tables strewn with rose petals, dimmed lighting and live *gnawa* music conspire to make this a venue suited to group conviviality or quiet intimacy. The menu isn't as sophisticated, but does offer above-average traditional dishes – *pastillas*, *tajines*, couscous – as well as a few pasta and pizza options. You can dine on fixed-price options or go à la carte. Perhaps the only real downside to Marrakchi is the service, which can be excellent, but on the wrong night can also be unforgivably nonchalant.

Food 7, Service 6, Atmosphere 7/8

● **Le Foundouk, 55 Rue du Souk des Fassi, Kat Bennahid.**
Tel: 0 44 37 81 90 lefondouk@wanadoo.net.ma
Open: noon–midnight. Closed Monday. 230dh

Traditionally, a *foundouk* was a 'resting-place' for tradesmen passing through town for the night. They would store their wares downstairs (the doors were locked) and get a night's sleep in one of the rooms upstairs. Most of them are now used as artisan workshops, but this one has been cunningly transformed into a

rather dapper restaurant by a pair of French furniture designers. In keeping with the old-style structure, it has three floors of galleries (including the ground floor) centred around a courtyard, which serves as a funky pre-drink/snack/lunch spot, with nifty décor and cool music. The first floor is *très chic*, arranged for intimate dining, while the highlight is the exquisite roof terrace, illuminated by candles at night and possessing sweeping views over the Medina. In keeping with the general ambience, the menu is innovative and elegant, with a mix of predominantly French and Italian dishes and traditional staples. With great service, a congenial ambience and value for money, this is definitely one of Marrakech's hotspots.

**Food 8, Service 9, Atmosphere 10**

**Hotel Les Jardins de la Koutoubia, 26 Rue de la Koutoubia, Medina.**
Tel: 0 44 38 88 00 www.lesjardinsdelakoutoubia.com
Open: 12–4pm and 7.30–10.30pm daily                    Price: 350dh

There are three restaurants at the Jardins de la Koutoubia, and all of them are worth a visit. On the ground floor, just off the reception, is the *restaurant gastronomique*, a refined space with an abundance of tables and formal décor that serves a range of sophisticated French dishes. It's a good place to eat if relatively busy, but when it's empty the size and starchiness can deliver a rather reserved experience. Next door, on the ground floor, is a new Moroccan restaurant which offers a selection of well-prepared local dishes. A more relaxed option in this instance is to head for the more intimate tables that skirt the pool, or alternatively climb the stairs to the romantically inclined Basque restaurant. This looks out over the Koutoubia Mosque and serves wonderful Spanish-influenced food and freshly prepared fish dishes. The price in both places is very reasonable, especially the lunchtime deals downstairs, which can be combined with a dip in the hotel pool if the management is feeling liberal.

**Food 8, Service 7, Atmosphere 7**

**L'Italien, Mamounia Hotel, Avenue Bab Jdid, Medina.**
Tel: 0 44 44 44 09 www.mamounia.com
Open: 8pm–midnight daily. Closed July and August.          525dh

L'Italien is the newest of the five restaurants located at the Mamounia and arguably the best. It is certainly the most stylish and intimate. Run by the pleasant host Lillian, the place is set (bizarrely) next to the hotel nightclub, though the two venues are kept thoroughly separate. Characterized by low ceilings, honey-coloured walls and a close-knit table arrangement, the restaurant is covered by a huge shallow dome, conjuring up a feeling of extravagance and indulgence – and that's before you set eyes on the menu. Tables are strewn with rose petals and the waiters make you comfortable as you browse the expensive-but-worth-it Venetian menu. There is a fantastic range of classic Italian fish, meat and vegetarian dishes, and the accompanying wine list must be the best in Marrakech, replete with famous and obscure French,

Moroccan and Italian selections, including a Chateau Petrus 1970, and a lesser known, locally produced Coteaux de L'atlas AOC.

**Food 9, Service 9, Atmosphere 9**

**Le Jacaranda, 32 Boulevard Zerktouni, Gueliz.**
Tel: 0 44 44 72 15 www.lejacaranda.com
Open: noon–3pm, 7–11pm daily                                        300dh

Le Jacaranda isn't an especially attractive proposition from the outside. The exterior is featureless and the location on the busy '4-Café' intersection along Mohammed V doesn't seem to promise too much tranquillity. However, inside is a decidedly charming space with food that far surpasses expectations in both quality and price. Owner/master chef Philippe Coustal (from Toulouse) has had the place for 15 years and has created an amicable interior that blends traditional elegant overtones with a quiet riot of lightly expressed purples and oranges. The menu boasts splendid French *nouvelle cuisine* as well as Moroccan and 'international' dishes, and has the option of set meals or plenty of à la carte options. There's an extensive wine list of local and European wines. The walls are covered with regular art exhibitions, which change every six weeks or so; and there is live music at weekends.

Food 7, Service 8, Atmosphere 8

**Jad Mahal, Fontaine de la Mamounia, Bab Jedid,
Hivernage.**
Tel: 0 44 43 69 84 palaisjadmahal@menara.ma
Open: 7.30pm–1am daily                                           350dh

Jad Mahal is part of a new breed of restaurants that has sprung
up in the last couple of years – a trend begun by Le Comptoir.
Their emphasis is on style and atmosphere as opposed to culinary excellence, but that's certainly not to say that the food is at
all poor. The brainchild of three French fashion designers, this
restaurant-cum-bar-cum-club has become the venue of choice
for society Marrakchi and wealthier visitors to town. The
Arabian–Indian décor, languid seating and exclusive atmosphere

is home to some fine Franco–Moroccan cooking. The menu is prepared monthly by Xavier Mathieu, a Michelin-starred chef and would-be Gary Rhodes who visits from France to discuss the menu with executive chef Vincent Faucher. As the evening wears on the wine flows, the music is pumped up, and then to tumultuous applause some of the finest (and most beautiful) belly-dancers in Marrakech arrive to liven up proceedings.

**Food 8, Service 9, Atmosphere 9**

**Le Jardin des Arts , 6–7 Rue Sakia El Hamra, Quartier Semlalia, Marrakech.**
Tel: 0 44 44 66 34 info@lejardindesarts.com
Open: noon–2.30pm, 7.30–11.30pm. Closed Monday lunch.
450dh

The eponymous garden that dominates Le Jardin des Arts is both capacious and captivating. Its wide chairs, large tables, good

sense of space and picturesque fountain make for a rather refined atmosphere. The 'art' part of the name becomes evident inside the main room, where local and international pieces (nothing overly controversial or exciting) hang from walls etched permanently with the names of famous historical figures such as Picasso, Ghandi and Newton. The owner – a Jewish fellow named Charles I Birroun – has created a menu that's as attractive as his premises, and which offers a range of decent French cuisine with fish, meat and vegetarian dishes available at reasonable prices. For 490dh you can try a little bit of everything, but the set lunch menus (sadly not on offer at weekends) are also excellent value.

Food 7, Service 8, Atmosphere 8

**Les Jardins de Gueliz, On the corner of Rue de la Liberté and Rue Tarik Ben Zayad, Gueliz.**
Tel: 0 44 44 62 38/0 65 97 48 62
Open: noon–2.30pm, 8–11.30pm. Closed Monday.        250dh

Les Jardins de Gueliz is a new spot in town, handily tucked away between the splendid Café Vittoria and boozy old Bodega. The

concept is an outdoor restaurant with tables located under bamboo roofing and grass-scratched *pisé* walls, looking out onto a large (700 square metres) and well-manicured garden, in which grow many of the aromatic herbs you may find on your plate. Owned by friendly French chef Jean-Baptiste, it offers mainly standard French cuisine with a few Spanish flourishes (the paella and calamari are good) and the obligatory Moroccan dish. There is a good-value set lunch price or you can go for à la carte options. The wine list is a little sparse, but there are enough Moroccan and international choices to keep you happy. In winter they close the glass partitions around the edge of the restaurant to ward off the chilly weather, creating a cosy and intimate atmosphere.

> **Food 7, Service 8, Atmosphere 7**

**Les Jardins de la Medina, 21 Derb Chtouka, Kasbah.**
Tel: 0 44 38 18 51 www.lesjardinsdelamedina.com
Open: noon–3pm, 7–11pm daily                              250dh

The resident cook, Najiz Hicham, has been here since the place opened two years ago and is a specialist in Nu-Moroccan cuisine. He's even written a book about it, and happily boasts that with 24 hours' notice he can produce any dish his customers want. The 'standard' menu (it changes every 2–3 months) certainly has a varied range of options from delicately cooked burgers and sandwiches at lunchtimes, to inventive local cuisine and a nothing-short-of-amazing 'Michael Bras style' chocolate tower in the evenings. Hicham is also known for his exquisite Thai dishes, though again with a day's notice. There are two main eating areas in the hotel: the seating around the pool is casual and suited to lunchtime while, inside, the restaurant is more formal and self-consciously styled but can still generate a convivial atmosphere. Since the hotel guests take priority, and since the more exciting food is available only with notice, it's worth calling ahead to make a reservation.

> **Food 7, Service 8, Atmosphere 8**

### Jemaa El Fna.
Open: 7–11.30pm daily                                          75dh

If you're feeling adventurous and want to eat in the most popular
'Marrakchi' style, sit at one of the sizzling food stalls in the nocturnal Jemaa El Fna. After dark the place becomes a giant open-
air barbecue as locals set up their stalls – illuminated by strings
of light-bulbs – and start harassing passers-by to sample their
wares. It's a superbly photogenic sight viewed from an upper terrace of a nearby café or restaurant, but the up-close experience
is really something else. There's not a great deal of difference
between one stall and another in terms of quality, but some sell
things that others don't. You can get anything from fried fish,
kebabs and salads, to sheep's head, brains or steamed snails. It
might be worth eating where the most Moroccans are eating. If
you want to rejoice in Marrakech's ancient and modern sights
and smells, this is the place to do it. However, it may be better
to leave it until the end of your stay, just in case!

Food 6, Service 7, Atmosphere 10

### Ksar Char-Bagh, Palmeraie de Marrakech, Palmeraie.
Tel: 0 44 32 92 44   www.ksarcharbagh.com
Open: noon–2.30pm, 7.30–11pm daily                            650dh

Ksar Char-Bagh's restaurant is a masterpiece and undoubtedly one of the finest in the city. Each day young French chef Damien Durand, who studied under Robuchon, Ducasse and Herme, creates a superb menu based on fresh market ingredients and produce from extensive orchard and garden that has been created behind the hotel's swimming pool (the plan is to create an organic pantry for the restaurant). Lunch is a simple three-course set menu, while dinner is usually a more extravagant à la carte affair. The high-ceilinged dining room and floodlit terrace provide a perfect situation for a wonderfully romantic candlelit meal and, like the hotel, play host to a crowd of international jet-set. Booking is essential: you will not be allowed into the hotel without a reservation.

**Food 9, Service 9, Atmosphere 9**

**Ksar El Hamra, 28 Riad Zitoun Lakdim, Medina.**
Tel: 0 44 42 76 07 www.net-tensift.com/ksar-hamra
Open: 8pm–midnight daily                                    450dh

Ksar El Hamra is one of only a handful of Moroccan restaurants where locals will go and spend their hard-earned cash instead of dining at home. There are two menus – the 'Gastronomique Sud' for 400dh and the 'Privelege Marrakech' for 450dh – the difference being that the latter has *Marrakech tajine*, a local meat dish that's slightly different from the usual *tajine* options. Inside, the restaurant is palatial with ornamentation dating back to the 19th century. The attraction lies in the large open courtyard, which ensures a memorable dining experience on warm evenings. The size of the place allows for large groups, but there are also smaller alcoves available if you want to make sure you avoid the coach crowds. At night there is entertainment in the shape of *gnawa* musicians and oriental belly-dancers.

**Food 8, Service 8, Atmosphere 8**

**Le Lounge, 24 Rue de Yougoslavie, Gueliz.**
Tel: 0 44 43 37 05
Open: 11am–1am daily                                               250dh

Le Lounge is a trendy new spot in Marrakech, a fact underlined by its self-consciously modern interior – a very red, very art-deco-inspired space that aims to make customers feel both

stylish and comfortable. The main dining space is small but is supplemented by an upper terrace level (where a DJ spins an agreeable mix of chilled sounds each night) and an outdoor area, both of which have couch-style seating and double up as bar hang-outs. The food is a congruous mix of Italian and French cuisine, not overly *haute* but tasty enough and well presented. There is a good spread of French and Moroccan wines and cocktails on offer to wash it all down. The bar is tiny, although at the time of writing there were plans to install a much larger American-style bar downstairs, which would make it even more appealing to the hip crowds.

**Food 7/8, Service 7, Atmosphere 8**

**La Madrage de St Tropez, Place du Petit Marche, Route de Targa, Gueliz.**
Tel: 0 44 44 79 79
Open: 6pm–midnight daily                              250dh

If you like Brigitte Bardot you're going to love this place. The owners are friends of hers, to which the multitude of pictures on the wall bears witness, and they set up this restaurant as a tribute to the legendary lady. You can find her everywhere: on the champagne bottles, on the menu, on the walls, and even on the stereo. You half expect her to serve your food, but instead that's down to the friendly and casual waiters. The venue opened

at the end of September 2002 (right next door to Pizzeria Niagara) and specializes in – *quelle surprise* – food from the St Tropez region, which can be very rich but is truly imaginative and tasty (the house aubergine starter is definitely worth trying). The décor is fairly flashy but not too ostentatious and there is a small bar inside where you can relax, before or after your food.

**Food 7, Service 8, Atmosphere 7**

● **La Maison Arabe, 1 Derb Assehbe, Bab Doukkala, Medina.**
Tel: 0 44 38 70 10   www.lamaisonarabe.com
Open: noon–2.30pm, 7.30–11pm daily                    400dh

Part of the hotel, La Maison Arabe's restaurant does not have the stunning visual impact that so many of the Moroccan establishments tend to have – there are no gurgling fountains, *zellijed* walls or strewn rose petals; instead a simple but quiet dignity prevails. What is on offer, which is rare in the Medina, is high-quality à la carte local food – the better 'palace' restaurants tend to have fixed menus with limited choice, which although delicious can be a little restrictive. A range of *tajines* and couscous dishes make up the menu and, while they can be quite conservative in what they offer, they are superbly cooked and full of flavour. As one would expect from this famous name the service is exemplary and scurrying waiters are always on hand to refill your wine or water glass. After dinner pop through to the bar,

Le Club, and enjoy another Marrakech rarity — a well-made cocktail.

Food 8, Service 8, Atmosphere 8

**Mamounia Moroccain, Mamounia Hotel, Avenue Bab Jdid, Medina.**
Tel: 0 44 44 44 09 www.mamounia.com
Open: 8–11pm daily                                     620dh

Not perhaps the finest Moroccan restaurant in town but certainly one of the best known, thanks to Alfred Hitchcock, who shot his film *The Man Who Knew Too Much* here. It happens to be a gen-

uinely attractive location for dinner too, with a main room covered in carved stucco and Venetian chandeliers, and another circular room set in Mamounia's art-deco style at the back, surrounded by an expanse of glass windows. The place seats around 130 people between the two rooms, so on busy nights quite an atmosphere can be generated, especially when the music gets louder and the oriental dancers come out to play. The menu is à la carte, full of traditional favourites and reasonably priced. There's a rather delicious *mechoui* available for two people at 700dh. If you come for dinner take a stroll in the hotel's fabulous gardens first.

Food 8, Service 8, Atmosphere 8

**Le Pavillon, 47 Derb Zaouia (opposite Bab Doukkala Mosque), Medina.**
Tel: 0 44 38 70 40
Open: 7.30pm–midnight. Closed Tuesday.　　　　　Price: 375dh

Le Pavillon is without doubt one of the premier places to dine in Marrakech. Shockingly simple yet stunningly effective, it has had a grand reputation for years, ever since the celebrated chef Philippe Cluzel, also the owner, added to its exquisite intimacy with a menu of innovative French cuisine. Recently, it has been

taken over but the place still remains peerless, and is good enough to attract Cluzel back for dinner. The main space is an elegant outdoor courtyard with tables squeezed in among the trees, and cosy salon alcoves around the sides. There's an upstairs space, too, which contains more stylized furnishings as well as comfortable sofas and chairs that encourage post-dinner relaxation. There's an emphasis on French-style meat and fish dishes (all seafood is bought up each day from the coast to maintain maximum freshness), with a few imaginative twists. The exquisite results and romantic setting make dining here an unforgettable experience. Sometimes tricky to find, they leave a man beneath the sign on the road to guide you into the restaurant, just in case.

**Food 8, Service 8, Atmosphere 9**

**Pizzeria Niagara, 31–32 Centre Commercial El Nakhil,
Route de Targa, Gueliz.**
Tel: 0 44 44 97 75
Open: 12.15–2.15pm, 7.15–11pm. Closed Monday.                    200dh

It might not be much to look at from the outside – just a run of
fence covered in foliage with a great big sign on the roof – but
Niagara is right up there alongside Catanzaro as one of the better Italian restaurants in Marrakech. The rest of the place is basic
but cheerful, with tables arranged outside on a patio (along with
a tragically 1980s Niagara Falls billboard) and inside in a spacious
room that's clean and comfortable. Most of the time these tables
are full, as tourists and locals alike flock to get their fill, a particular favourite of the ex-pat community. There's not only excellent
pizza and pastas but a good range of Italian fish and meat dishes
as well. The high quality of the food, decent prices and unpretentious charm easily explain the popularity of the place. It's a short
ride from central Gueliz (10dh or so in a taxi) and definitely
worth the effort.

**Food 8, Service 8, Atmosphere 8**

**Puerto Banus, Rue Ibn Hanbl (opposite the Royal Tennis
Club), Gueliz.**
Tel: 0 44 44 65 34 www.restaurantpuertobanus.com
Open: noon–3pm, 7.30–midnight daily                    240dh

Puerto Banus is a Spanish-themed seafood restaurant run by a Moroccan family. The outdoor courtyard is romantically lit at night by the gentle glow of luminous fish tanks and strips of fairy-lights that cascade down one wall. Off the courtyard are inviting internal alcoves for colder nights or more personal dining. Insouciant Latino music tinkles away as you sip sangria and ogle the tortillas and paella, and mouth-watering oddities such as Mexican *brochettes* and curried fish dishes on the menu. The food

can sometimes be on the heavy/rich side but is generally good. The place attracts a mixed clientele, with everyone from middle-aged tourists to locals and young couples enjoying the down-to-earth but appealing ambience.

**Food 7, Service 8, Atmosphere 7**

**Riad Tamsna, 23 Derb Zanka Daika (off Riad Zitoun El Jdid), Medina.**
Tel: 0 44 38 52 72 www.tamsna.com
Open: 10am–midnight, daily; *tapas* is served 6–8pm.          350dh

Riad Tamsna, hidden among the dense alleyways of Zitoun El Jedid, was the first venture of the Loum family, who bought the place in 1989 and opened it several years later as a stylish, high-end restaurant. It was restored by renowned local designer Meryanne Loum-Martin, daughter of the family, whose inventive flair is immediately evident, with designer furnishings, elaborate wall-hangings, exhibitions along the first-floor gallery and fashion boutique all providing not just an elegant setting but shopping options to boot. The main restaurant is on the ground floor with a slew of tables and an alcove out back for private or intimate dining. The food is every bit as stylized as the venue: a hip mixture of fusion cuisine that includes Spanish *tapas*, Moroccan and French dishes, and seafood, all tailor-made for the environment. There's also an array of fine cocktails on offer that can be sam-

pled on the relaxing roof terrace, where the odd DJ has been known to spin a slick selection of grooves to the funky clientele.

**Food 8, Service 9/10, Atmosphere 9**

**Les Terraces de l'Alhambra, Place Jemaa El Fna, Medina.**
Tel: 0 44 42 75 70
Open: 7am–11pm daily                                    150dh

The slick, canopied exterior of Les Terraces is fairly conspicuous by the square's modest standards and is obviously a recent appearance. Run by a trio of Frenchmen, it markets itself as a fairly cosmopolitan pizza/pasta restaurant as well as an ice-cream and snack parlour. There's a ground floor with outside seating perfectly positioned to view the endless hustle-bustle of the Jemaa El Fna, and two floors upstairs for eating, both of which have air-conditioned interiors and outdoor terraces with expansive views. The service is suave and alongside the usual run of *tajines* and couscous are some more friendly pizza and pasta dishes. A traditional set menu will set you back 120dh or you can plump for a Menu Alhambra (salad, pizza/pasta, dessert) for just 95dh. Standards can be a bit hit and miss, although mostly the dishes are above average and occasionally even excellent. They also serve breakfast until 11am; lunches and dinners are available anytime.

**Food 6, Service 7, Atmosphere 7**

**Le Tobsil, 22 Derb Abdellah Ben Hessaien, R'mila Bab Ksour, Medina.**
Tel: 0 44 44 15 23
Open: 7.30pm–midnight. Closed Tuesday.                    600dh

Tobsil (meaning 'dish' or 'plate' in Arabic) is located deep inside the Bab Laksour area (look out for the signposts for Riad Catalina: Tobsil is next door). It's an elegantly restored *riad* house owned by Christine Rio (whose grandmother was a chef from Brittany) and her photographer husband. Tobsil is reckoned by many to be the best eating establishment in Marrakech and, while that may be arguable, it certainly resides in the upper echelons of the city's gastronomic scene. The intimate ambience mixes with the exquisite food and excellent service to

create an unmissable experience. Inside the *riad*, tables are placed around the plant-filled courtyard, in smaller salons and around an upper gallery level. Soft music, sensuous candles and liveried staff create an idyllic atmosphere which is matched by the glorious food – traditional but refined – that bears down on you as soon as you've settled in, and doesn't stop until way after your belly has started begging for help.

**Food 9, Service 9, Atmosphere 9/10**

**La Trattoria Di Giancarlo, 179 Rue Mohammed El Bekal, Gueliz.**
Tel: 0 44 43 26 41 www.latrattoriamarrakech.com
Open: 7.30–11.30pm. Closed Sunday and lunchtimes.          425dh

Arguably the finest Italian restaurant in town, La Trattoria combines an incredibly romantic ambience, crazy décor (courtesy of local American hero Bill Willis), exquisite Italian food and exemplary service all in one place. Having been open for 20 years it has had a bit of a head start on the rest in terms of getting things right, but you can't knock the fact that everything happens remarkably well here. The entrance, courtyard and grand salon all bear Willis's surreal signature: stripy chimneys, beguiling ornamentation and quirky detailing. The main dining area is in the garden, where candles bob sensually in a pool, casting a soft glow over the nearby tables. All you have to do is sit and relax as waiters dressed in pinstriped suits bring you refined Italian food (nouveau and traditional dishes) and cater obsequiously to your every whim. It's not cheap but it is fantastic.

Food 9, Service 10, Atmosphere 9

**Trois Palmiers, Mamounia Hotel, Avenue Bab Jdid, Medina.**
Tel: 0 44 44 44 09 www.mamounia.com
Open: noon–3pm daily                                                375dh

Trois Palmiers, another of the Mamounia's restaurants, is famous for its buffet-style lunches, which are served up and eaten either under the shade of the hotel's large tree-lined swimming pool or

in the white canvas *caidal* tent (traditionally used to welcome *caids*, or local dignitaries). The setting is undeniably pleasant and the food – a vast range of salads, steaks, chops and seafood (all chargrilled) plus Moroccan dishes and lots of tasty pastries, desserts and cheeses – is similarly pleasing; if you don't know what to eat, the waiters will choose a selection for you. One of the main attractions is being able to check out the grounds of the hotel without spending an arm and a leg on a room – the gardens are certainly worth a stroll. During July and August, lunch is à la carte.

**Food 8, Service 8, Atmosphere 8**

# drink...

Alcohol is officially frowned upon in Muslim culture, but that doesn't seem to stop anyone drinking if they really want to. Morocco's drier than most Western places, of course, but less so than many Islamic countries because of its laid-back attitude to things.

There isn't exactly a plethora of bars in Marrakech, but there are a few. Many are annexed to restaurants or hotels since it's easier to get an alcohol licence that way; this tends to cultivate a certain formal atmosphere. However, there are several independent bars, which are mainly found in Gueliz.

The Medina, as you might expect, given its status as the more traditional part of the city, isn't exactly overrun with places where you can enjoy a cold beer, but piano-style hotel bars such as Mamounia and the Hotel Les Jardins de la Koutoubia offer pleasant surroundings, and restaurants such as Tamsna, Le Pavilion and Le Lounge provide salons/spaces for pre- or post-dinner drinks.

Most of the nightlife takes place out in Gueliz where you can find some intriguing – if run-down – local drinking holes (Musica Bar,

L'Escale, Café Atlas), as well as a selection of slicker bar/restaurant-style venues. La Casa, Montecristo, Bodega and Le Comptoir are the most notable examples of this latter category; all attract locals, tourists

and that particular brand of young woman – familiar the world over – who, with the right combination of eye contact and body language, will accompany you at the bar and allow you to buy her drinks.

The music in these latter places tends to be a loud mix of R&B, rap, Latino and Oriental/Arabic sounds, sometimes joyously raucous, occasionally downright annoying.

Alcohol is expensive in most places, though more so in nightclubs than bars. The average price to pay in bars is around 30–50dh for a beer or a glass of wine and 50–80dh for a cocktail.

For cheap draught beer and good old-fashioned, down-to-earth fun, try Bodega; for an intimate chat and quieter ambience, opt for a hotel bar like Churchill's or Zanzibar, or, for lovers of chic, there is the roof terrace at Montecristo or the unapologetic opulence of Le Comptoir. If you want to combine food and loud music, La Casa is the place for you.

**Bodega, 23 Rue de la Liberté, Gueliz.**
Tel: 0 44 43 31 41
Open: 12pm–3pm and 7pm–2am daily

In Spain a *bodega* is a cave. In Marrakech, Bodega is a Spanish-themed *tapas* bar, a cheap, easy-going place that sells draught beer and lends itself to DJ-fuelled cacophony. It's one of the few places that is genuinely popular with locals and ex-pats alike (Wednesdays have become English/American night) and is always likely to be lively. The clientele range's from giggling teenage girls and beer-hugging boys to canoodling couples and even families. The *tapas* is cheap, but basic; the décor is brash (red painted chairs, bullfighting posters, football scarves), there's draught beer and a TV screen flits between fashion and sports channels. The French owners take pains to make everyone feel comfortable and welcome. The best time for a relaxing beer is between 7 and 11pm; after that the

volume is turned up, though there is also a peaceful courtyard cantina outback to escape into.

**Bô-Zin, Douar Lohna, Route de l'Ourika 3.5km.**
Tel: 0 44 38 80 12 www.bo-zin.com
Open: 8pm–1am daily

As a restaurant it can be slightly hit-and-miss in the gourmet stakes, but for sheer entertainment it is without fault. The bar proves a good option, therefore, especially after dinner. In the summer everyone mixes together, lounging languidly on large cushions under a canopy as flaming torches illuminate the night sky; in winter, you can sit inside on the banquettes enjoying a glass of whisky in front of a roaring fire. The energetic, atmospheric interior makes an effective contrast with the tranquillity of the Moroccan garden outside, and at weekends be prepared for dancing around, and possibly on, the tables. Bô-Zin's location slightly out of town has its plus and minus points: you'll need a taxi to get here (and although they're quite cheap, this can be a hassle), but it has no neighbours to upset, so the bar can stay open as long and late as the party continues.

**La Casa, Hotel El Andalous, Avenue President Kennedy, Gueliz.**
Tel: 0 44 44 82 26
Open: 7pm–2am daily

If neon *tifinigah* (Berber lettering), loud music and good international food are your thing of a night-time, then La Casa could be the bar for you. Located right next to the Hotel El Andalous, this is a popular place where Moroccans as well as tourists come to drink, whoop and make merry to the usual mix of club-heavy tunes. A circular bar dominates the sizeable space and provides the only non-table seating. The rest of the place is ostensibly a restaurant, with groups and couples dining, cuddling and preparing to boogie as the night wears on. The menu offers a mix of Spanish, Mexican, French, Italian food, which isn't exactly *haute* but is tasty enough. You can choose smaller *tapas* versions of many dishes for 35dh or get a full plate for around 65dh. Happy hour is usually between 7 and 10pm, when you can buy two drinks for the price of one.

**Churchill's Piano Bar, Mamounia Hotel, Avenue Bab el Jdid, Medina.**
Tel: 04 44 44 44 09 www.mamounia.com
Open: 5pm–1am daily

Dress smartly if you want to get into this place or the sniffy doormen won't let you in. Part gentleman's club, part jazz club, the interior is designed in a classic art-deco-meets-jazz style – soft leather chairs and wall-coverings, a semi-private drinking room off the main bar area, a grand piano in a shallow pit, and runs of bar stools. This is all gently illuminated by backlit painted glass that features colourful pictures of famous jazz legends

and can look spookily ecclesiastical after a couple of the right drinks. You'd be forgiven for thinking the place was kitted out along with the hotel in the 1920s but in fact it was refitted during the 1980s refurbishment. Still, the ambience seems to work. The bar opens at 6pm each night, plays music (jazz) from 9pm and sells classic whiskies, long drinks, draught and bottled beer and cigars. It's often very quiet but occasionally surprisingly busy, particularly when the film festival is in town.

**Le Comptoir, 37 avenue Echouhada, Hivernage.**
Tel: 0 44 43 77 02 www.ilovemarrakesh.com/lecomptoir
Open: 5pm–1am Monday–Thursday; noon–1am
Friday–Saturday

Le Comptoir is more famous as a restaurant than as a bar, but the latter area – located upstairs from the main restaurant – is an elegant and passionate place to go for a drink. In fact, the locale's glamorous and trendy reputation, sleek design and funky atmosphere may well make it more appealing than many other more 'dedicated' bars around town. It's decked out in the same manner as the restaurant – curvaceous, stylish, low-lit, comfortable – and you have the benefit of hearing a more considered mix of music here than elsewhere. In keeping with the essence of the place, the drinks aren't cheap, but they're not that much more than other hotspots, plus the bar is well stocked and the service is good. You can also slink back down the stairwell and out into the garden courtyard if you prefer some horizontal cushion-lounging.

**Jad Mahal, Fontaine de la Mamounia, Bab Jdid, Hivernage.**
Tel: 0 44 43 69 84  palaisjadmahal@menara.ma
Open: 7.30pm–1am

Part of the Jad Mahal restaurant/club empire in Hivernage, this is one of the few places to catch discerning local cognoscenti supinely reclining in armchairs and sipping gin and tonics or a cool glass of champagne. Like its neighbour and competitor Le Comptoir, Jad Mahal provides a sophisticated environment for a relaxing drink,

particularly pre- or post-dinner. Entrance is restricted, and unlike many of its competitors in Gueliz the bar is not full of 'working girls', or too many elderly tourists clutching guidebooks, camera bags and fanny packs. As the night wears on it begins to fill up with diners wanting an extra drink before they head downstairs to the club. Alternatively there's a rooftop terrace overlooking the city walls to one side and out towards the desert on the other, which makes a wonderfully romantic place to sip a cocktail once the sun goes down.

● **La Maison Arabe, 1 Derb Assehbe, Bab Doukkala, Medina.**
Tel: 0 44 38 70 10  www.lamaisonarabe.com
Open: 5pm–11am daily

La Maison Arabe seems to have answered one of the Medina's oldest questions: where is a good place to go

for a drink? A new bar, opened by the hotel's Italian prince owner, was originally designed as a jazz bar, but at the time of writing it was struggling to pull in the evening clientele. The interior has been designed with a central African–sub-Saharan theme with dark wooden furniture and carved bas-reliefs hanging from the wall. A sophisti-cated cocktail list and tempting *tapas* menu indicate the right intent in an area otherwise devoid of drinking estab-lishments. Like the hotel, Le Club is imbued with an air of

quiet sophistication as well-to-do couples indulge in a
glass of champagne before dinner or a swift nightcap. At
the moment the problem is that the bar closes at 11pm,
just as some are leaving the neighbouring restaurants and
could do with one more before weaving their way
through the moonlit streets of the Medina to bed.

### Montecristo, 20 Rue Ibn Aicha, Gueliz.
Tel: 0 44 43 90 31
Open: 8pm–1am daily

At the time of writing Montecristo was the most popular
spot in town with both tourists and the local cognoscenti.
It's a relatively smart bar for Marrakech, with three different levels: a restaurant downstairs serves up good pasta
and pizza dishes; a middle Cuban-themed floor provides
late-night disco action; while the exotic roof terrace functions as a pre-nightclub bar. Since most people come here
towards midnight for the middle floor, the upstairs is usually quite empty, which makes it perfect for a relaxing
drink. A very funky spot it is too, with low-lit candles and
hookah pipes on tables arranged around the perimeter of
the roof, all under cover of a tent-like canopy and amid
decorative foliage. The roof has its own bar that's surprisingly well stocked, offering tasty cocktails, cigars and even
bites of pizza (made in the restaurant downstairs). On a
warm night, it rocks, and if later on you fancy busting

some flash moves or indulging in some unencumbered hedonism, just wait until after 11pm when you're only one floor away from a dramatic change of atmosphere.

**The Piano Bar, Hotel les Jardins de la Koutoubia, 26 Rue de la Koutoubia, Medina.**
Tel: 0 44 48 88 00
Open: 7pm–midnight daily

The Piano Bar, situated just inside the Jardins de la Koutoubia hotel, is a pleasantly low-key spot for a drink. In contrast to the rest of the fairly restrained and traditionally decorated ground-floor salon rooms of the hotel, the bar is an assertive combination of reds, blacks, yellow

and beiges with a vaguely darkened ambience that borders on louche. There are red stools lined up at the bar, with bow-tied staff attentively awaiting orders, comfortable sofas and a crooner playing the instrument that gave the bar its name (though he's handy on a synthesizer too). There's no dress code to speak of but the bar overtly aims to attract five-star clientele; it's doubtful you'll be staying long unless you look smart and are happy to notch up a decent bill. The bar is rarely busy, making it the perfect place to enjoy a quiet drink and a more private chat.

Zanzibar is being touted as the hot new *tapas*/bar in Marrakech, although in reality it's the old Tikida Gardens piano bar, 'Nawas', transformed and now featuring a spread of comfortable red sofas, chairs and low tables, a splendorous wooden bar that gently calls from the corner and a regular DJ who plays unobtrusive music each evening. It has almost done away with the previous bar's hotel undertones – but not all of them. There's still an air of formality about the place that prevents it from ascending into the league of the achingly hip, though with a distinct lack of options in Marrakech it certainly isn't a bad place to enjoy a drink. The drinks are relatively cheap, with cocktails at 45–70dh, beers 25–45dh (including draught beer). The *tapas* does exist but it's more of a ruse to secure a liquor licence. Most problematic, perhaps, is the location, out in the Palmeraie (100dh each way in a taxi), so we'd recommend combining a visit with use of the hotel's extensive spa or maybe dropping in for a drink before going on to the New Feeling nightclub, located not far away at the Palmeraie Golf Palace (see page 136).

Updates and notes...

# snack...

Café culture as we know it in the West doesn't really exist in Marrakech. There are certainly plenty of cafés around town, and they serve a similar social function to our own, but the difference in levels of comfort, design and gender balance is acute.

In Marrakech the preference is for austere, functional places that are decorated with obligatory pictures of the king, serve mint tea, thick black espressos, the odd croissant and…not a lot more. Fortunately for lovers of cappuccinos and lattes a few places have cropped up in the last couple of years. Proprietors have begun to recognize the potential profit to be made from creating a more welcoming atmosphere, and expanding the choice of food and drinks until it resembles something approaching an actual menu.

The venues below vary. Some, like Vittoria, are heavily Westernized; others are elaborate patisseries that have made good (Adamo, Al Jawda) or slick hotel-connected spots such as Sunset and Boule de Neige. Both Amandine and Café Arabesque are comfortable local haunts. Literary cafes, like Dar Cherifa, provide a quiet, calm and cool place in the Medina to sip coffee or mint tea surrounded by decent art and a sense of well being.

Many of these cafés are good for breakfasts and/or lunches, but be warned that a number of them still only provide a coffee, a congenial atmosphere or a fattening pastry. Speaking of breakfasts, you might like to try out a traditional Moroccan one, which consists of – surprise, surprise – lots of sweet things such as the doughnut-esque *sfinge*, or *bghrir* (a pancake made with yeast) and *msama*, as well as a selection of hot pancakes with butter and honey.

One of the joys of Marrakech is the abundance of fresh oranges found everywhere. Walking through the Jemaa El Fna can be a rather heated experience, but take the time to stop and have a glass of freshly squeezed orange juice at one of the many stalls; or simply pick up some dried fruit to munch on the move.

In the early evening it might be nice to stop at one of the more anonymous cafes within the Medina and enjoy a glass of mint tea while you unwind with a hookah pipe stuffed with apple tobacco – a true Arabic tradition.

**Adamo, 44 Rue Tarik Ibn Ziad, Gueliz.**
Tel: 0 44 43 94 19 www.traiteur-adamo.com
Open: 8am–1pm, 3.30–8.30pm. Closed Sunday afternoon and
Monday.

Adamo is ostensibly just a shop-front for French chef Bruno's
catering service, which supplies all kinds of functions, from wed-
dings to conferences and birthdays, with his tasty homemade
treats. The shop itself is bright, clean and small, with tables out-

side on the pavement and a coolly air-conditioned interior that
can serve as a welcome refuge from the dusty streets of Gueliz.
It's a little light on offerings, with just a smattering of mini-*brochettes*, chocolates, sandwiches, croissants and quiches displayed
on its refrigerated glass shelves. Best used as a neat little coffee
and snack stop-off if you're shopping in the area, rather than
somewhere to head for a substantial lunch.

**Al Jawda, 84 Avenue Mohammed V, Gueliz.**
Tel: 0 44 43 46 62 www.al-jawda.com
Open: 8am–9pm daily

There are two Al Jawdas. There's the ultra-cute patisserie on the
Rue de la Liberté, which has been supplying Marrakech and
Morocco with tasty treats for 18 years. Then there's the larger
sister-store, more of a sit-down event on Mohamed V, just

opposite the restaurant Chez Jack'line. It's a family operation, with mother (Mrs Alami) taking care of the Liberté café and son (Aziz) managing this one, which is justifiably famous among locals. Excellent sweets and pastries (which are on display in tall glass refrigerators), large cappuccinos, great milkshakes, a good selection of breakfasts (international included) and sweet and savoury crêpes are all much in demand. The traditional interior adds to the local/family-run atmosphere, though most people grab a chair out front where they can people-watch in comfort.

**Amandine, 177 Rue Mohammed El Bekal, Gueliz.**
Tel: 0 44 44 96 12
Open: 6am–11pm daily

If it's clean, safe, cake-based fun you're after, look no further than Amandine. A bright, light and tight *patisserie/salon de thé/gelateria*, it comprises two sections. The part to the right of the entrance – polished and shiny – offers tasty cakes, sweets and ice creams, and has an endearing collection of tiny toy giraffes behind the counter. You can chew on a peach Melba or a *dane blanche*, or grab a *pain au chocolat* or *toast fromage*. Slightly more relaxed (especially for smokers) is the café proper next door, which has stools and seating, more decoration, a spot of music, and a con-genial atmosphere. It has the same range of food and drink

options and there's an upstairs gallery to complement the main room.

**Askmy Cyber Café, 6 Boulevard Zerktouni, Gueliz.**
Tel: 0 44 43 06 02
Open: 24hrs daily

One of the attractions of Askmy, located just along from the Cinema La Colisée, is that it offers speedy broadband internet connections for those who don't want to spend hours of their holiday waiting for slow phone lines to download. There are 15 or so computers, plus a couple of points for those who want to add their own laptops to the network. It's also one of the only internet places that functions as a café as well. You can order a

drink and a snack (though nothing more substantial than a piece of cake or a croissant) in the less sterile area upstairs. Staff are young and friendly so it's no real surprise, given that it's open all through the night, that it has become a bit of a cool hang-out for the young locals (mostly male).

**Boule de Neige, Rue de Yougoslavie, Place Abdelmoumen, Gueliz.**
Tel: 0 44 44 60 44
Open: 5am–11pm daily

Next to the Hilton's eye-wateringly delicious patisserie, Boule de Neige offers a darkened green and pink interior and a pleasant

sunny patio with wicker chairs shaded by umbrellas. The only real food – apart from the sticky bun collection near the counter – is breakfast (continental 30dh, American 50dh) served between 8 and 11am, although the patio is a good spot to grab a drink anytime. The staff couldn't care less if you have a nice day but despite the sullen service they don't mind if you pop next door and bring back a pastry or two. There is an upstairs salon, which is about as inviting as the frumpy downstairs section.

**Café Arabesque, Avenue Mohammed V, Residence Al Mourad, Gueliz.**
Tel: 0 44 43 98 50
Open: 6am–11pm daily (breakfast 6–11am)

Located on the busy Avenue Mohamed V, Arabesque is a little-known but delightful haunt in which locals like to take refuge from the searing heat of the day. It consists of a pretty little garden area outside with wrought-iron furniture and a tiny decorative bridge leading to a two-tiered indoor space that's air-conditioned and pleasant to relax in. The venue opened four years ago and has its fair share of regulars who come to enjoy the ambience along with a breakfast, snack or coffee. The menu is fairly broad, with a selection of breakfast options, sandwiches, *paninis*, pizzas and salads for a more substantial feast. There's a good choice of ice creams and milkshakes, too.

### Café de France, Jemaa El Fna, Medina.
Open: 6am–11pm daily

Café de France doesn't go big on decorative chic but nonetheless it's one of the best-known places on the Jemaa el Fna. Its large dimensions and excellent location make it a convenient meeting-point, and ensures that it's always busy with a healthy mix of locals and tourists. There is a lunch and dinner menu but the food isn't particularly inspiring and the service is usually whimsical at best. We recommend you take the short walk to such restaurants as Terraces d'Alhambra, La Marrakchi or even Chez Chegrouni next door. What does make it worthwhile, however, is the open terraces where you can go for a drink and a convivial chat, and the top floor especially affords great views over the square.

Café les Negoçiants, 110 Angle Ave Mohammed V et
Boulevarad Zerktouni, Gueliz.
Tel: 0 44 43 57 82
Open: 6am–11pm daily

A curious question raised by Café les Negoçiants, an attractive
and cosmopolitan café in the centre of Gueliz, is this: why would
you bother spearing a toastie with a cocktail stick when all there
is to keep inside is a slice of processed cheese – and not a particularly bulky one at that? Such burning issues are unlikely ever to
be addressed, but it doesn't really matter because the reason to
come here is not the food (although the breakfasts are decent);
the strength of Negoçiants is its terrific social ambience. In fact, it's

massively popular with locals, many of whom recline on the rattan seating out front, watching the action on the perpetually busy Abdel Moumen from beneath the distinctive green and white awning. The clientele is mixed, too, especially for Moroccan cafés, which are usually male-dominated. Business folk, gay crowds, families and hipsters all warm to Negoçiants' wide appeal.

### Café Palais El Badii, 4 Rue Touareg Berrima, Bab Mellah, Medina.
Tel: 0 44 38 99 75
Open: 8am–10pm daily

Overlooking the noisy but attractive Place des Ferblantiers, where workers beat metals into saleable shapes, the Palais is admittedly not the most peaceful café in the world. But the constant chink-chink of the artisan's hammers is remote enough not to be invasive as you sit on the upper terrace amid the tradi-

tional Moroccan lamps and zellije-covered tables and enjoy the views. It's one of the few places in the area that offers set lunches (choose from the 'El Bahia', the 'Marrakech' or the 'Tafraout', all of which include salads, soups, fruit, tea, coffee and biscuits and a main tajine or meat dish) for 60dh. There are no set breakfasts but plenty of breads and croissants available. A peculiarity of the place is that the sign outside plainly advertises sandwiches;

yet asking for one will provoke a look of bewilderment or a knowing smile.

### Café Vittoria, 21 Rue de la Liberté, Gueliz.
Tel: 0 44 43 15 29
Open: 7.30am–midnight daily

By far the most comfortable (and Westernized) coffee-stop in town, Vittoria is a chic little haunt, with soft purple chairs in a *tadelakt*-walled main room, and tables and chairs positioned around an attractive adjoining courtyard. The first thing that assails the senses is the freezer just inside the main door, which is full of authentic Italian ice cream available in a startling range of colours and flavours. The main menu is much more extensive than most places in town, boasting everything from sweet and savoury crêpes, salads, a choice of set breakfasts including an 'American' with buttered toast and cornflakes, *paninis* and of

course lots of variations on the ice-cream theme. In fact the most expensive thing on the menu is the 'Royal', a veritable vase-full of five ice-cream scoops.

### Dar Cherifa/Café Literaire, 8 Derb Charfa Lakhir Mouassine, Medina.
Tel: 0 44 42 64 63 www.marrakech-riads.net
Open: 9am–7pm daily

A splendorous oasis of calm in a crazy city full of smell and noise, Dar Cherifa has to be experienced at least once during a trip to the Medina. It is one of the most majestic *riads* in town, founded by Abdelatif Ben Abdellah (of Marrkech Riads fame – their offices are upstairs), who has transformed the place into an art gallery, library and general shrine to inner peace. Visiting the place, with its elegant columns, relaxation salons and Zen-like atmosphere, is like receiving an architectural massage. Exhibitions change every few weeks and vary in theme (and quality), but there is a permanent photography exhibit (upstairs) that documents the sensitive restoration of the space three years ago. There's also a small but perfectly formed library of books on Moroccan and French culture, and you can take a mint tea or coffee here for 20dh. A quintessential Moroccan experience.

**Nid' Cigogne, 60 Place des Tombeaux Saadiennes, Kasbah, Medina.**
Tel: 0 44 38 20 92
Open: 9am–9pm daily

An unprepossessing place (to say the least) from the outside, Nid' Cigogne is nonetheless a bit of a godsend, offering shaded respite and a good menu when the going gets hot down in the Kasbah. It's handily located opposite the Saadian tombs, the walls of which the local storks like to use as a meeting-place and

lavatory. After the initial ascent up the shabby staircase, you reach
a covered terrace that looks directly down on the entrance to
the tombs and the usually busy square around it. Behind is another, prettier roof terrace which uses plants and vines to good
effect, and a mezzanine level with a couple of wicker chairs set up
for an intimate chinwag. The menu is surprisingly extensive and
inexpensive. Choose from such dishes as vegetarian couscous, salads, *tajines*, omelettes, and hot and cold soups. Those with a sweet
tooth and a keen eye for cakes will have probably already spotted
the convenient neighbouring patisserie on the way in.

### Patisserie de Princes, 32 Rue Bab Agnaou, Medina.
Tel: 0 44 40 30 33
Open: 5am–11pm daily

Patisserie de Princes is possibly the most famous sweet shop in
Marrakech, located on the budget-traveller strip known as the
Rue Bab Agnaou, leading just off the Jemaa el Fna. It's the place
to head if you are enamoured with all things sugary and pow-
dery and/or partial to the occasional delicious milkshake. It's also
very convenient if you simply want to dive out of the heat and
into somewhere coolly air-conditioned. The front of the shop is
full of cakes and pastries, all temptingly laid out in chilled glass
cabinets. Once you've bought your treats you can pass through

to the popular back room or up to the *grand salon*, and mingle with the locals and tourists while the ubiquitous pictures of the king stare down at you from the walls.

**Restaurant Mer Langouste, Corner of Mohammed V and Rue Soriya, Gueliz.**
Tel: 0 44 43 85 54
Open: 9.30–midnight daily

You can't really miss this place if you're walking along Mohamed V – the curvaceous sign is large enough to compete against the cinema billboards next door. It's a newish place (opened in 2002) and, as the name suggests, specializes in seafood. It could be classed as more of a restaurant than a café but it serves sizeable dishes all day and has chairs outside for customers who just require a drink

or a snack. The place takes a typically Spartan approach to furnishing but is clean and spacious inside and comfortable enough to promote relaxation. The menu has salads and fishily themed main courses such as *tajines*, paellas, *brochettes* and spaghetti with *fruits de mer*. The chef lived in the USA for 10 years specializing in fish dishes, which may explain the quality of the food.

**Sunset, Palmeraie Golf Palace, Palmeraie.**
Tel: 0 44 30 10 10 www.pgp.co.ma
Open: 9.30am–5pm, 6pm–midnight daily

Sunset is one of the newer additions at the sprawling resort that goes under the name of the Palmeraie Golf Palace. It's pretty far out of town, and in the evenings becomes more of a dinner spot rather than a café, but we've included it here because it makes a great place for lunch. The food is fairly standard – sandwiches, salads, *brochettes* and pizzas – but it's located right next to a gorgeous, fun-shaped pool (to which you have access, if you're dining, for an extra 150dh). The ambience is pleasant and breezy, in line with the structure of the place, which consists of loose-flowing pieces of plastic sheeting that flap gently back and forth against relaxing black and white sofas. The complex also boasts activities that can keep you occupied for an entire day, such as golf, tennis and horse-riding. There's a bar that sells alcohol, and for those still there in the evening, Sunset has a superior dinner menu. At 11pm it turns into an outdoor party – with New Feeling situated literally over the road.

# party...

Marrakech's nightspots are a direct extension of the bar scene. There is an abundance of 'hotel' nightclubs but they usually mostly range from uninspiring to downright alarming. The best clubs are listed below. They have been chosen because they offer a good mix of tourists and locals, a more contemporary (if not overly diverse) spread of music, and can be a lot of fun on the right night.

As with the bars, most of the good nightclubs are located in Gueliz, although New Feeling is out in the Palmeraie. There is another similarity with the bar scene: a barely concealed sex industry exists, so men should be aware that girls who show an interest will usually have money rather than romance on their mind.

Many of the nightclubs share a similar music policy (which is suspiciously akin to what the bars tend to play), and the interiors are laid out in much the same way, with a large, main dance-floor overlooked by a circular terrace where you can have a drink and watch events unfold.

The price of drinks in the clubs is high by European standards: 50–90dh for a beer and 90–110dh for a cocktail is quite normal. If you are with a few people

it might make sense to purchase a bottle from the bar in advance and keep it on the table; this usually gets the admission charge waived (usually between 100–150dh, often including a drink) and so can work out cheaper.

Unfortunately there are upsettingly few places to witness live music in Marrakech. Venues such as VIP and other small, local places occasionally put on traditional Oriental cabaret, which can involve mini-orchestras and talented singers and dancers covering popular and classical songs from the Arab world. More often than not, however, it consists of a man with trousers tightened far too high above his waist, warbling dramatically over a selection of synthesized Casio beats.

For the more fiscally adventurous, the casinos also offer alternative late-night entertainment. The best and more interesting ones are at the Mamounia and Es Saadi hotels. The Mamounia is far more glamorous inside, while the Es Saadi has a spectacular exterior with flames leaping from the centre of the fountain. One can bet with relatively small stakes so don't feel too in awe of the places.

## NIGHTCLUBS

**Diamant Noir, Hotel Marrakech, Place de la Liberté, Avenue Mohammed V, Gueliz.**
Tel: 0 44 43 43 51
Open: 11pm–4am daily

Every place has its institutional dive, and Marrakech has the Black Diamond. Actually, it's unfair to call it a dive, although it certainly doesn't meet the ice-cool standards of the other bars. It's more of a no-frills nightclub of the kind found all over the world, yet it still attracts plenty of young locals who drum up a vibrant atmosphere, especially at weekends. You can feel the slightly jaded edge of the place as soon as you walk through the distinctly unglamorous entrance and down into the two-tiered

discothèque proper. The top-floor bar (where the 'ladies' often gather and collectively preen, perched on stools) has some comfortable seating, DJ booth and a couple of pool tables in case it's a really dull night. Downstairs is dominated by the mirrored dance-floor, more seating and another couple of bars. Diamant Noir also forms part of Marrakech's flourishing gay scene and it can be a pick joint for those of either sexual preference. Not one of the most happening clubs in town, especially considering its undertones.

**Jad Mahal, Fontaine de la Mamounia, Bab Jdid, Hivernage.**
Tel: 0 44 43 69 84 palaisjadmahal@menara.ma
Open: midnight–5am Thursday–Saturday

The third part of the Jad Mahal empire is its über-chic club, the pet project of Jean Jacques Garella (one of the three *fashionistas* who own the place). He enjoys an elevated position in the French fashion hierarchy, and the interior shows more than a passing interest in the work of Versace. Purple and leopard-skin abound, with specially designed double stools/sofas behind the bar a unique feature. Determined to keep the 'working girls' at bay, they claim to let in only one in five who approach the velvet ropes. The clientele are the wealthy and the glamorous who come to dance the night away free from sleaze and intrusion. Currently an in-house DJ works the decks playing a mixture of house and club classics, but there are moves afoot to introduce some more well-known international names. At present the club has plans to expand to every day of the week.

**Montecristo, 20 Rue Ibn Aicha, Gueliz.**
Tel: 0 44 43 90 31
Open: 11pm–1.30am

The roof terrace might be relaxed and intimate, but come 11pm the middle floor of Montecristo comes alive and Marrakech's nightlife begins in earnest. Largely speaking, this is the place to be for much of the city's youthful fraternity. It's the floor where the Cuban theme is most pronounced, not just because it sells cigars, but also because there are Che Guevara posters behind the bars, the barmen wear Panamas and serve up tasty *mojitos* and the occasional member of staff has been known to break into spontaneous bursts of lively salsa dancing. Of course it's a very thin veneer, but Montecristo is nonetheless busy enough most nights to create a good atmosphere. There's not a great deal of seating, so get settled early if you don't want to be standing, and witness many of the attractive local girls plying their trade. The upstairs remains open in case an escape route is required.

**New Feeling, Palmeraie Golf Palace, Palmeraie.**
Tel: 0 44 30 10 10
Open: 11pm–3.30am daily

Perhaps it's the fact the crowds have some excess cash, maybe it's just the buzz of a hot new nightspot, but the fact that New Feeling is way out in the Palmeraie doesn't seem to deter anyone from going. It costs 100dh each way but since it has the reputation for being the best place in town and attracts a lot of the city's cognoscenti it's largely worth it (taxi drivers, without fail, recommend it as the place to be – but they would, wouldn't they?). The venue attempts to pitch itself at an up-market crowd, and is in the same league as Jad Mahal and Theatro (with whom it competes for best venue in town). Tell-tale signs are the Lichtenstein and Haring prints on the walls, and the plethora of shirts and trousers as opposed to jeans and sneakers. The main dance-floor has a ritzy glass podium for the principal movers and shakers and space enough for anyone else who wants to join in. The crushed-glass bar is a nice touch though the prices aren't quite so cool. There are lots of the obligatorily curved seats around the dance-floor and an upper gallery that's normally fairly empty. If you are staying in the Palmeraie at one of the sophisticated villa/palace/kasbah hotels, then this is your best option for a late night drink.

**Paradise, Kempinski Mansour Eddahbi, Avenue de France, Hivernage.**
Tel: 0 44 33 91 00
Open: 10.30pm–4am daily

Paradise is one of the flashier clubbing locales in town, popular with wealthy locals and ex-pats alike. It's bigger than most of the other clubs with a 1,500 capacity, and is characterized by a clutter of sparkling lights and ostentatious decoration. There's a staircase that sweeps heroically downstairs to the main bar area, a large dance-floor overlooked by a state-of-the-art DJ box, lots of intimate and comfortable seating and table arrangements (which fill up as the night wears on: they can be reserved in advance), and an upper terrace that features a massive video screen on one side and a perpetually deserted salad bar on the other. As the night draws on, power-dressed men cavort increasingly with under-dressed 'ladies' to the familiar sounds of R&B, hip-hop and Arabic music. Occasionally the place gets carried away with itself and a less self-conscious atmosphere emerges.

**Theatro, Hotel Es Saadi, Avenue El Quadissia, Hivernage.**
Tel: 0 44 44 88 11
Open: 10pm–4am daily.

The man who started the Es Saadi hotel – Frenchman Jean Bauchet – once managed the famed Moulin Rouge in Paris. After building a casino then a hotel here, he also built a theatre and put on not just plays but also musicians such as Dizzy Gillespie.

The theatre closed down a few years ago but was opened at the end of 2002 in its new guise as nightclub, overseen by Bauchet's grandson Jean-Alexandre. The place has had an up-market refurbishment, giving the interior a much more modern look (with designer furniture, strategically placed tables and a large and very expensive bar), while retaining its original structure. On our first visit the place was literally erupting in an atmosphere of uproarious hedonism with people lounging around on four-poster beds on the stage, staff pouring drinks over each other while dancing on the bar and a DJ playing the latest club tunes on a superb sound system. At weekends Theatro can become seriously packed, you can book a table in advance which comes with a bottle of spirits – at a substantial cost of course. Alongside Jad Mahal this is the place to be seen on the weekends at the moment. Housed beside the casino, the plethora of top-of-the-range sports cars parked outside testifies to the kind of clientele who frequent the club.

### VIP, Place de la Liberté, Avenue Mohammed V, Gueliz.
Tel: 0 44 43 45 69
Open: 10pm–4am daily

This place used to be known as Star's House, but they ripped the inside apart, refurbished it and renamed it VIP. Seemingly it has done the place wonders, as it's gone from being regarded as a mediocre venue into an excellent place for a night out. Any nervousness provoked by the somewhat precocious neon tunnel that leads downstairs should be disregarded. As soon as you take a right turn into the venue proper you find what is perhaps the closest Marrakech gets to a normal nightclub. There's more neon, a swish new bar and lots of seating downstairs. The DJ seems to know his house and techno music in a little more depth than the others and often whips his visitors into a frenzy. Turn left down the aforementioned tunnel and you end up in a quite different scenario, a world of Moroccan cabaret where musicians passionately play strings and synths, and singers and dancers entertain a mostly local crowd. You can sashay happily between the two rooms but management somewhat meanly prevent you taking your drinks in between. Make sure you visit when you have some energy and you'll find a fun and varied night under one roof.

## CASINOS

**Es Saadi, Avenue El Qadissia, Hivernage.**
Tel: 0 44 44 88 11 www.casinodemarrakech.com
Open: 4pm–4am daily

The Es Saadi casino, situated 50 metres from the hotel, has an old-fashioned air in keeping with the nostalgic feel of the hotel itself. The hotel remains a family-run business and grandmother can still be found counting up at the end of the night. The facilities inside the vast space are up to date with video slot

machines next to more traditional games like craps, stud poker, punto blanco, blackjack and roulette. On Fridays you can enjoy a traditional meal with a Moroccan 'spectacular' beforehand.

**La Mamounia Casino, Mamounia Hotel, Avenue Bab Jdid, Medina.**
Tel: 0 44 38 86 44/43 www.mamounia.com
Open: 4pm–5am daily

La Mamounia's vast, vaulted casino has a slightly faded opulence that some might consider charming. The cavernous interior is more reminiscent of Vegas than it is of Marrakech. It has obviously seen many fortunes won and lost, and has played host to some worthy gamblers. Here the well-heeled Marrakchi mix with the international jet-set to create an expensive and rarified atmosphere. There is a separate restaurant and bar area, and the main hall is set up for roulette, blackjack, poker and baccarat as well as more than a hundred gaming machines. Be warned, you will not be allowed in if you are untidy, and that I'm afraid means no blue jeans or trainers.

# culture...

Marrakech's principal allure stems not from a plethora of monuments and museums, but from its sights, smells and sounds which are consistently compelling, particularly to Western senses.

The best way to sample the real flavours of Marrakech is to wander the mazy streets of the Medina, where there seems to be a new surprise to take you back in time round every corner (if there's one thing Marrakech doesn't lack, it's corners). And a few hours spent people-watching on the Jemaa El Fna will likely be memorable – day or night.

There are plenty of historical, novel and interesting sites to visit: the Koutoubia, the Saadian Tombs, the Ben Youssef Medersa, the Marrakech Museum, the Badii Palace and Dar Tiskiwin are all aesthetically and culturally rewarding.

The Koutoubia stands out on Marrakech's skyline, visible from most points in the city, and occasionally a marker point to those lost in the back alleys of the Medina. On the other hand the Marrakech Museum, although well signed, can be difficult to find for a Medina novice, tucked away in the back streets.

Visiting the historical sites can be frustrating: the Koutoubia is only open to

Muslims, so most westerners can but admire the tower from the outside; and the Agdal Gardens are only open at weekends, except for those when the king is in residence.

Marrakech's gardens provide oases of calm within the often hectic city. The Majorelle Gardens,, owned by Yves St Laurent, offer a marked contrast with the hustle and bustle of a busy working city in Gueliz while the Mamounia Gardens are similarly refreshing in the Medina.

Although the town seems to be full of ex-pat designers, photographers, painters, sculptors and film-makers, the local arts scene remains sparse. The visual arts and literature tend to be dominated by past masters, but a younger and exciting scene is starting to emerge (check out the Matisse and Bleue galleries for examples of fresh Moroccan painters).

The Marrakech Film Festival, inaugurated in 1999 and held every year, is a cause of celebration for the town and the largely international coverage that has followed has helped give the city a more artistic and cosmopolitan image.

## SIGHTSEEING

**Badii Palace, Place de Ferblantiers, Mellah, Medina.**
Open: 8.30–11.45am, 2.30–5.45pm daily. Admission: 10dh

What was once part of a sumptuous palace, built by Ahmed El
Mansour in the 16th and 17th centuries, is now just a smattering
of battered ruins. So opulent was the palace that it reportedly
took 25 years to complete. A hundred years later, however, it
was raided and all the treasure sent elsewhere. Nowadays, it's
pretty stark. There isn't even a gate, just a hole in one of the
palace walls, which leads into a vast area dominated by sunken
spaces that once housed flourishing gardens and a grand reflecting pool, but which still contains a few trees. There are also some
excavated remains of caves and passages and some well-
weathered original floor mosaics. Apart from that it's just you,
your imagination, and the storks that use the battlements as latrines.

**Bahia Palace, Riad Zitoun El Jdid, Medina.**
Tel: 0 44 38 92 21
Open: 8.30–11.45am and 2.30–5.45pm daily. Admission 10dh

The Bahia Palace was originally constructed by the infamous
vizier Ba Ahmed Ben Moussa in the early 1900s. When he died it
was inhabited by the French *resident-generaux*, and is today used

for a range of purposes – King Mohamed VI famously threw a party here for US rap star P. Diddy in 2002. The palace is undeniably elegant, with grand columns, stucco and *zellije* galore throughout the main areas and countless bedrooms that used to house Ben Moussa's numerous 'other halves' (four wives and 24 concubines, to be exact).

**Ben Youssef Medersa, Place Ben Youssef, Medina.**
Tel: 0 44 39 09 11/2
Open: 9am–6pm. Admission: 20dh

A *medersa* is a Koranic school, specifically built for the teaching of Islamic law and scripture. This particular one was built in the

14th century and enlarged to its present size in 1564. It is in remarkable shape, primarily because it was still in use up until the 1960s, and it's a stunning place to visit. A long corridor leads into a large, tranquil central space with a pool. At one end of the room is a prayer closet, in which lecturers delivered their lessons, backs to their audience to make use of the dome's echo-friendly acoustic structure. Around the central courtyard are scores of ascetic, cell-like rooms, which were used as student quarters.

## Jemaa El Fna
Medina

All roads seem to lead to the Jemaa El Fna so you're bound to visit it at some point. Though it's dubbed the 'square' it's actually

an irregular 'L' shape that is as old as the city itself. A vivacious display of local life and colour night and day, it is largely untouched by Western influences and maintains traditions that stretch back a thousand years. Daytime in the square is relatively restrained – by night-time's raucous standards. From the many cafés that surround the action, you can watch a smattering of snake-charmers, scribes, tattooists, musicians and beggars sit or hobble around while covered wagons, arranged in a grand semi-circle, offer freshly squeezed orange juice. Come sunset, the music grows louder and events gather pace as story-tellers, potion-sellers, magicians, acrobats, dentists, transvestite dancers and other assorted mystical figures join the party, and a thousand and one food stalls are set up to create one of the most photogenic barbecues in the world.

### Koutoubia Mosque
Jemaa El Fna, Medina

Paris has the Eiffel Tower, London has Big Ben – and Marrakech has the Koutoubia Mosque. Towering over the square (and over the whole of the Medina), it's the highest point in the city by a long way and the landmark with which visitors become most acquainted. '*Koutoubia*' means 'of the booksellers', and the mosque acquired its name because of the profusion of book-traders that used to gather around. The main structure was built

in 1158 but the minaret was added later by the architectural enthusiast Yacoub El Mansour. Unfortunately it's only the outside you'll be seeing unless you're a Muslim, and that from a slight distance, since non-Muslims are barred from the interior and most of the surrounding areas.

### Saadian Tombs, Rue de Kasbah, Bab Agnaou, Medina.
Open: 8.30–11.45am, 2.30–5.45pm daily
Admission: 10dh

The Saadian Tombs are located right next to the Badii Palace.
They're small in size but large in cultural significance given that
they contain the sacred mausoleums of the sultans of the
Saadian era. The tombs were discovered by accident in the 1920s
by the French military. The low, mosaic tombs inside pre-date the
Saadian era. The main attractions are three pavilions, which
include a Prayer Hall and the Hall of Twelve Columns, containing
the tombs of various Alaouite princes plus the Saadian sultan
Ahmed El Mansour, and his son and grandson.

## GALLERIES AND MUSEUMS

**Dar Tiskiwin, 8 Rue de la Bahia, Medina.**
Tel: 0 44 38 91 92
Open: 9.30–12.30pm, 3.30–5.30pm daily
Admission: 15dh

Dar Tiskiwin is the concept of Dutch anthropologist Bert Flint. A
keen collector of Berber antiquities from rugs and tables to jewellery and clothing, he decided a few years ago to open up his
private treasures to the public. They are housed in a typically
labyrinthine *riad*, which still acts as his home. A permanent exhi-
bition includes an imaginary 'trail' along the old nomadic caravan
routes and offers information on – as well as cultural artefacts
from – sub-Saharan tribes that are not really mentioned in

writings or oral traditions, with the aim of preserving the cultures of these communities.

**Musée d'Art Islamique, Majorelle Gardens, Avenue Yacoub El Mansour, Gueliz**
Open: daily, 8am–noon, 3–7pm in summer; 8am–noon, 2–5pm in winter
Admission: 15dh. No children. Dogs and picnics forbidden.

The inviting, boldly blue building in the Majorelle Gardens is the Museum of Islamic Art. It used to be the studio of Jacques Majorelle (who gave the gardens as well as the blue colour his name) but was renovated into a neat little space displaying all kinds of artefacts and decorations relating to Islamic art. Through several small rooms, a range of Irke pottery, polychrome plates,

jewellery, antique doors and other assorted exhibits are displayed.

**Musée de Marrakech, Place Ben Youssef, Medina.**
Tel: 0 44 39 09 11/2
Open: 9.30am–6pm daily
Admission: 30dh

Back in 1997 the government renovated this grandiose 20th-century house into an impressive gallery space, and it's thus a dual attraction. There's the building itself, which consists of a network of different-sized rooms that have been converted into show spaces, yet whose design – such as the immense UFO-style chandelier in the main hall – and decoration are absorbing. Then there are the exhibitions, all temporary, which focus on 'heritage' art in the central hall, and contemporary art in the *douiria* and *hammam*. There is also a neat little café just near the door which comes in very handy in hot weather.

## GARDENS

**Agdal Gardens, Royal Palace, Medina**
Open: sporadically, but usually at weekends. Closed when the King is in residence.
Admission: free

These gardens were built in the 12th century during the Almohad dynasty. Located at the back of the Royal Palace, they comprise vast (40-acre) gardens and orchards that incorporate pomegranates, figs, oranges, walnuts and vineyards. There are some pavilions scattered around but the showpiece of the gardens is a huge pool right in the centre, which was once used for swimming practice by the sultan's soldiers and claimed the life of at least one sultan.

**Majorelle Gardens, Avenue Yacoub El Mansour, Gueliz.**
Open: daily, 8am–noon, 3–7pm in summer; 8am–noon, 2–5pm in winter; daily.
Admission 20dh. Dogs and picnics forbidden, no children.

The Majorelle Gardens are today owned by Yves St Laurent but were primarily the project of French artist Jacques Majorelle (son of celebrated furniture maker Louis Majorelle), who opened them to the public in 1947. The collection of plants was started in the 1920s, imported from five continents in order to create an overwhelmingly exotic jumble of floral exotica. Palms, cacti and bamboo all thrive in this small but enchanting place, amid attractive walkways, a lilied pool, and the Museum of Islamic Art. Walking through the gardens is akin to walking through the Eden Project with every different plant annotated for the visitors' information and the keen gardener can spend hours sitting in the shade admiring the prime examples of the different species.

**Mamounia Gardens, Mamounia Hotel, Avenue Bab Jdid, Medina.**
Tel: 0 44 38 86 00 www.mamounia.com

The Mamounia (see page 50) actually takes its name from its gardens, which are over a hundred years older than the hotel, constructed by Prince Moulay Mamoun in the 18th century. The gardens aren't huge but the orange trees, olive trees, colourful flowerbeds and assorted flora are all meticulously maintained and create a positively charming environment for a stroll. It's best to dress a little smartly and it might also be worth combining your visit with a buffet lunch at Les Trois Palmiers (see page 104) or an afternoon tea to guarantee admission.

**Menara Gardens, Avenue de la Menara, Hivernage.**
Open: 5am–6.30pm daily
Admission: free. Picnic pavilion 15dh

The Menara Gardens consist of a large basin of water surrounded by fertile orchards. The water basin goes back to the 12th-century Almohad era, though the green pavilion (which affords great views of the basin from the first floor) was added in the 19th century. You can spot the carp swimming in the water, stroll in the orchards or picnic in the pavilion. Come night-time, the

place hosts a fantasia – with 'spectacular' 3D colour re-enactments of famous historical battles.

## CINEMA

**Colisée, Boulevard Mohammed Zerktouni, Gueliz.**
Tel: 0 44 44 88 93
Admission: 15–25dh Monday; 25–35dh Tuesday–Sunday

There are several cinemas in town, but Colisée is the best by far. It's a spacious place with comfy seating, a decent-sized screen and a stream of conveniently placed cafes nearby for pre- or post-movie lounging. The selection of films on offer is normally imported mainstream blockbusters and usually shown in French with Arabic subtitles.

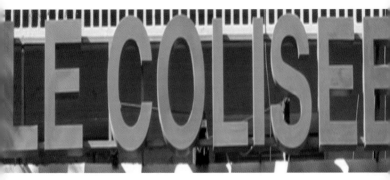

# shop...

Prolonged retail exploration in Marrakech usually provokes equal amounts of surprise and frustration. Shopping here is an art form. The souks (markets) have proved the inspiration for many professional and amateur interior designers.

The souks (located just off the Jemaa el Fna) represent the most famous shopping 'precinct', and are a must even if only to sample the unique atmosphere. Set in a maze of intricate Medina-style alleyways, the shops (there's rumoured to be 1,000 of them) range from shallow kiosks no bigger than broom cupboards to tiny storefronts that miraculously morph into huge warehouse-style spaces.

Traditionally the souks were divided into different areas – one for metalwork, one for leather, one for carpets, and so on. Although there has been a certain degree of cross-pollination over the last few years, these areas can still be vaguely discerned. Here, you can purchase everything from *baboush* (pointy leather slippers that come in an array of garish colours), carpets, kaftans and *djellabahs* (traditional Muslim attire for men and women), lanterns, leather goods…and, yes, even camels. There's plenty on offer, although the compact structure of the markets and speedy skills of the local artisans mean that anything that sells well gets replicated almost immediately and hence many stalls offer exactly the same things.

The customary bargaining process in the souks can be unpleasant or fun, depending on the attitude of the trader and your own philosophy on such things. If you don't like haggling, then go along to one of the artisan centres listed below where prices are fixed (well, as fixed as they're going to get in Morocco). In fact, it might be an idea to visit one of these before the souks, to get an idea of the average price of things. If you are going to haggle, do it with a smile – a knowing wink will get you a lot further than a po-faced grimace. (And that goes for dealing with Moroccans generally: even the most hardened hustler can give way astonishingly easily to a more human spirit, willing to converse amiably. Our rule on haggling means starting at about one-third of the price that you are initially quoted and ending up at about 50%. You still might end up over-paying but at least you'll be close to a good price.) Be aware, too, that no matter how low the price you achieve, it's very unlikely it'll be a huge bargain as Moroccans are all too aware of the real value of their goods. Be especially careful when being sold 'antiques' – the majority are not authentic.

Those who seek something other than traditional wares will be delighted to hear that there is a fairly pervasive designer scene in Marrakech, doubtless a spin-off of the burgeoning chic *riad* culture. Such stylish boutiques can be found in the Medina though the majority are in Gueliz, where shopping is a more European affair generally. Along the New City's wide boulevards is a variety of clean and spacious shops selling everything from traditional and designer clothing to funky furniture, antiques, home accessories, leather goods, imported footwear and jewellery.

Hours of shopping vary. As a rule places seem to be open between 9am and 6pm Monday to Saturday, but these guidelines – and even some of the times listed for each individual store below – should be taken with a pinch of salt as proprietors often exercise their right to open and close when they want.

There is no provision for tourists to reclaim any sales tax or VAT on accommodation or goods that they buy. Many traders in the smaller shops actively resist giving an official receipt, since this forces them to declare (and thus pay) VAT.

## THE SOUKS

The Souks provide Marrakech's, and indeed most of the Arabic world's, legendary shopping experience. Known to hold almost anything that visitors might possibly want from carpets to candlesticks, *djellabas* to toothbrushes.

Found in the area to the north of the Jemaa el Fna, the souks can be incredibly intimidating to the novice. Sometimes leaving a trail of breadcrumbs seems logical – narrow alleys twist and turn branching off to the left and right – if you ever want to find your way out again.

The souks used to be compartmentalized by product and in a way still are, although today carpets, leatherware and spices sit side by side. One should start off by heading north from the Jemaa el Fna on rue Fehi Chidmi up to Mouassine Mosque, then head right along Souk Labadine Attarine before turning right down Souk Nejarine and into Souk Semarine which leads back to the Jemaa el Fna. If you follow these routes you will come across everything that you need to see.

For the more adventurous turn off these main lanes to either the left or right and visit the smaller *derbs* and markets. Alternatively keep heading north past the Ben Youssef Mosque and wander the alleys here. These are far more authentic and where the real Marrakchi live and trade – instead of carpets and *baboush* expect worked metal, fresh herbs and butchers. The

tourist trade is less in evidence; instead the roads are full of everyday artisans at work. This is where you will pick up the real smells, sights and sounds of the Medina.

One of the most frustrating aspects of shopping the souks is knowing that you are paying over the odds. If you are really serious about your shopping we recommend asking the owner/manager of your *riad* to accompany you, or provide you with a guide; this should stop you being taken for a ride. Alternatively learn to barter, and barter hard. We have had experiences of being offered products at 300dh for a pair of baboush, bargained hard and taken them for 50dh, but still known that we are paying over the odds. Roughly half of the original asking price seems to satisfy most.

## ANTIQUES

● **Dar Bou Ziane, 20–21 Rue Sidi El Yamani Ksour, Medina.**
Tel: 0 44 44 33 49 darbouziane@iam.net.ma
Open: 9am–7pm daily

This place touts itself as an art gallery (which it is, with changing exhibitions that showcase local painters), but its primary function is an 'antique' shop. It stocks an incredible amount of traditional furnishings and large-scale objects such as Berber doors, giant candlesticks, fireplaces, ceramics and jewellery.

**El Badil, 54 Boulevard Moulay Rachid, Gueliz.**
Tel: 0 44 43 16 93
Open: 9am–7pm daily

El Badil offers only the most authentic of antiques. Over two floors you can find a glittering display of ancient treasures that include Fez ceramics, Berber doors, mirrors, rugs, carpets, chests…and the list goes on. Brad Pitt and Hillary Clinton are just two of the visitors here, though it's a surprisingly down-to-earth place.

**L'Orientalist, 11 and 15 Rue de la Liberté, Gueliz.**
Tel: 0 44 43 40 74 F: 0 44 43 04 43 orientaliste@wanadoo.net.ma
Open: 9am–12.30pm, 3–7.30pm Monday–Saturday;
10am–12.30pm Sunday

L'Orientalist boasts a vast selection of modern and antique goods (it works with over a hundred local artisans) across two stores, located just along the road from one another. The larger shop holds most of the outsized delights, but between them they offer all kinds of artistic creations, paintings, perfumes, antiques, ceramics, marble, wood, enamelled glassware, textiles, clothes, cushions, plus modern clothing and designs and much more. A must for all budding designers.

**La Porte d'Orient, 9 Boulevard Mansour Eddahbi (next to Glacier Oliveri), Gueliz.**
Tel: 0 44 43 89 67
Open: 9am–7.30pm Monday–Saturday. Closed Sunday.

At first sight this place look like every other antique shop, but make an appointment with the owner and you'll be shown a huge back room full of very genuine – and very expensive – antique artefacts. The front store specializes in wood but has jewellery, lamps, manuscripts, thrones and fountains to boot.

## ART GALLERIES

**Gallerie Bleu, 119 Avenue Mohammed V, Gueliz.**
Tel: 0 44 42 00 80 g.bleue@menara.ma
Open: 10am–1pm and 4–8pm. Closed Monday.

A recently opened space, small but fresh, Le Gallerie Bleue is the project of local artist Chalal, who displays his own semi-abstract daubings amid those of other Moroccan and international artists. Chalal is of Berber origin, a fact represented in his symbolist paintings that blend traditional religious motifs with Miró-esque shapes and colours.

**Marrakech Arts Gallery, 60 Boulevard Mansour Eddahbi, Gueliz.**
Tel: 0 44 43 93 41 www.art-gallery.marrakech.com
Open: 9am–1pm, 3–8pm daily

This place is the sister gallery of La Qoubba and exhibits primarily the same stuff – which is to say the predictable run of traditional paintings with little space retained for more interesting modern material.

**Matisse Gallery, 61 Rue de Yougoslavie, No 43 Passage Ghandouri, Gueliz.**
Tel: 0 44 44 83 26 matisse_art_gall@hotmail.com
Open: 9.30am–1pm, 4–8pm daily

The Matisse Gallery is a space dedicated to showcasing both old and modern Moroccan artists. It is owned and carefully maintained by Youssef Falaki and Youssef Nabil Moroccan (both artists themselves) and has several up-and-coming young artists on commission who have built up an impressive selection of lively, hip canvases. Makes a refreshing change from seeing ubiquitous Orientalist works.

**Ministero del Gusto, 22 Derb Azzouz El Mouassine (off rue Sidi El Yamami), Medina.**
Tel: 0 44 42 64 55 www.ministerodelgusto.com
Open: 10am–1pm, 4–7pm. Sunday by appointment only.

Designers Fabrizio Bizzarri and Alessandra Lippini (formerly style editor for Italian *Vogue*) opened their 'Ministry of Taste' a few years ago. It's a breathtaking space, a feast of curves, crazy artwork and imaginations gone wild. Within the wilfully wobbly walls is a range of furnishings and decorations made by the owners and their designer and artist friends from around the world, who contribute pieces that are often as madly creative as the space that they inhabit. Three times a year the gallery hosts music and art exhibitions.

**La Qoubba, La Qoubba Gallerie d'Art, 91 Souk Talaa, Medina.**
Tel: 0 44 38 05 15 www.art-gallery-marrakech.com
Open: call for details.

Close by the Musée de Marrakech, this prominent space is full of bright but fairly predictable canvases. There doesn't seem to be a lot to get the pulses of contemporary-art lovers racing, but if its classic and 'modern' Orientalism you seek then it's a safe bet you'll find something to buy here.

## ARTISANS' MARKETS

**Centre Artisanal, 7 Derb Baissi, Kasbah, Medina.**
Tel: 0 44 38 18 53/0 44 38 19 73 tapisantiquite@iam.net.ma
Open: 8.30am–8pm daily

Located just along the road from the Saadian tombs, this is one of the most popular shopping spots and certainly one of the biggest. A vast, impersonal space, it stocks literally everything you could think of: handwoven rugs, Berber jewellery, antiques, teapots, home and garden furnishings, slippers, suitcases, kaftans and bejewelled daggers. It's soulless but convenient and although it says no haggling, 'discounts' are available, especially if you buy a few items.

**Centre Commercial, 3 Residence El Habib, 65 Boulevard El Mansour Eddahbi, Gueliz.**
Tel: 0 44 43 92 58
Open: 9am–7pm daily

Centre Commercial is a large space choc-full of assorted goods. It's not as well known as the other two and doesn't seem to stock quite as much, but prices are more negotiable and there are still plenty of useful purchases to be had. The staff do occasionally try to fleece their customers, however, so be aware.

**Ensemble Artisanal, Avenue Mohammed V, Medina.**
Tel: 0 44 38 67 58
Open: 8.30am–7.30pm daily

Similar in style and appearance to the Centre Artisanal, this place sells a similar range of goods and products (that is, everything from antique guns to leather suitcases). The added allure of the Ensemble is that it's state-owned, so all the products on display are supposedly there by royal decree and thus the best of their kind.

## DESIGNER CLOTHING

**Adolfo de Velasco, Mamounia Hotel, Avenue Bab Jdid, Medina.**
Tel: 0 44 44 59 00
Open: call for times.

This little shop located in the Mamounia is as stylish as you'd expect. It's run by Dr Velasco, a famously colourful character who designs incredible kaftans for women. The store also sells random pieces of art and antiques.

**Amanjena Boutiques, Route de Ouarzazate, Km 12.**
Tel: 0 44 40 33 53
Open: 10am–7pm daily

There are three boutiques at the luxurious Amanjena hotel. They all sell accessories supplied by the Aman Resorts head office, but also wonderful designer clothes, fabrics, jewellery and candles by

the likes of Valerie Barkowski (**see** Mia Zia, page 164), Bridgette
Perkins, Amira and Amina Agueznay. It's a long way to go, of
course, but you might also like to visit the hotel's health spa,
have lunch in the pool-side restaurant or just admire the opulent
architecture and environs.

### Beldi, 9–11 Soukiat Laksour, Bab Fteuh, Medina.
Tel: 0 44 44 10 76
Open: 9.30am–1pm, 3.30pm–8pm daily

Beldi is one of the best-known boutique outlets in the city, even
if its scruffy exterior may suggest otherwise. Owned by two
Moroccan brothers, it specializes in subtly Westernized
Moroccan cuts for men and women, in a range of compelling
colours and mesmerizing materials. The collections change con-
stantly; drop by to see what they have on offer.

### Casa Mangani, 26 Rue Tarik Ibn Zyad, Gueliz.
Tel: 0 44 43 56 34 www.mangani.net
Open: 9am–1pm and 3.30–7.30pm. Closed Sunday, and Monday
afternoon.

If you don't know the famous Florentine porcelain called Mangani,
you will after visiting here. The shop is full of lamps made from
the stuff, pleasantly displayed throughout what happens to be a
groovy little show-space. The designs tend to veer between Italian
and Moroccan, and vary in shape, size and pattern, but are mostly
ornamental. What might prove more eye-catching for the mini-
malists are the furniture designs of architect/designer Soumaya
Jalal, who works with raffia, horse-hair and other materials to
produce low-key stylish wall-hangings, cushions, curtains and rugs
in pleasing whites, coffees and creams.

### Intensité Nomade, 139 Avenue Mohammed V, Gueliz.
Tel: 0 44 43 13 33
Open: 9am–12.30pm, 3–7.30pm. Closed Sunday.

The owner of this place – Frederique Birkemeyer – once owned the leather store Birkemeyer's (see page 171). This venue is a few notches up the style ladder, however, with a wealth of hip little kaftans, shirts, jackets and slippers on display, as well as other accessories. There is also a smattering of Moroccan designer Noureddine Amir's funky threads.

### Kulchi, 1 bis, Moul Laksour (opposite the Laksour Fountain), Marrakech.
Tel: 0 62 64 97 83 kulchimarrakech@hotmail.com
Open: 9.30am–1pm, 4–8pm. Closed Sunday.

A cute little space if ever there was one, Kulchi is half-hidden away just along from a herbalist on the corner of the Rue Mouassine. Inside are coolly contemporary clothes, bags and accessories with an antique twist, as well as such items as jewellery, T-shirts, shoes, perfumes and vintage *djellabahs*.

### Marion Theard, Dar Cannaria, 54 rue des Banques, Medina.
Tel: 0 44 42 66 09
Open: call for times

Marion Theard has been involved in Morocco's *'haute couture'* scene for a while but has only just opened her own place. Situated in her own *riad*, she boasts a neat selection of natty women's stuff, from *baboush* and throws to place-mats and bathing accessories.

### Mia Zia, 322 Sidi Ghanem industrial estate, Route de Safi.
Tel: 0 44 33 59 38 www.miazia.com
Open: 8am–6pm Monday–Friday; 8am–5pm Saturday

Mia Zia is owned by Valerie Barkowski, who runs several boutiques in Europe. This place is her factory showroom and is one of a few different reasons to head to the Sidi Ghanem industrial estate (about 30dh each way from the Medina). There are baboush and jumpers, shirts and socks and an assortment of non-clothing items – all for less than European prices.

### Michele Baconnier, 6 rue de Vieux, Gueliz.
Tel: 0 44 44 91 78 michelebaconnier@yahoo.fr
www.ilove-marrakesh.com/baconnier
Open: 9am–7pm daily

Tiny but impeccably stylish, this boutique is definitely worth a peek. Madame Baconnier excels at merging the traditional and the hip, and her outlet stocks a range of cool jewellery, clothing, *baboush*, handbags, candlesticks, rugs and soaps. There are some antiques here, too (furnishings as well as clothing), and even a cosy outside café to enjoy a spot of tea and lunch.

### Scenes du Lin, 70 rue de la Liberté, Gueliz.
Tel: 0 44 43 61 08 bluemajorelle@hotmail.com
Open: 9.30am–12.30pm and 3.30–7.30pm daily

Scenes du Lin is a striking, low-lit store run by French textile expert Anna-Marie Chaoui and her Moroccan husband. The original function of this place was as a showroom for her wonderful collection of natural fabrics, some of which, like *mlifr*, are local, while others are imported from around the world. The place also sells tablecloths, dressing-gowns, curtains, kaftans and bedspreads, plus snazzy furnishings and funky candles made by Laurence Corsin and Amira, respectively.

### Tamsna Boutique, 23 Derb Zanka Daika (off Riad Zitoun El Jdid), Medina.
Tel: 0 44 38 57 60 www.tamsna.com
Open: 10am–midnight daily

This funky little boutique showcases Meryanne Loum-Martin's designs among others, such as Brit jeweller Joanne Bristow and silk-scarf creator Paige Hartong Thon. There are hand-woven *djellabas*, cool kaftans, smooth raffia and cotton, cushions, bedclothes, stylish *baboush* and many other things that squeak with chic.

## FOOTWEAR

**Artika, 70 Prince Bab Agnaou, Medina.**
Tel: 0 44 44 16 93
Open: 9am–1pm, 3–9.30pm daily

A good spot for shoes and loafers ranging from formal to smart-casual. It brings a wide range of imported brands, such as Caterpillar to Morocco, and it also sells belts, socks and other accoutrements.

**Atika, 34 Rue de la Liberté, Gueliz.**
Tel: 0 44 43 64 09 atikab@iam.net.ma
Open: 8.30am–12.30pm, 3pm–7.30pm. Closed Sunday.

There is another Atika in town (down the road at 212 Mohammed V), but this is the biggest and most popular. It does a fine line in chic and stylish footwear (shoes, boots, sandals, sneakers, etc., for men and women) in a range of local and international styles.

## HOME DECORATION

**Amira, 522 Lot El Massaur, Route de Safi.**
Tel: 0 44 33 62 47 amirabougies@hotmail.com
Open: 9am–1pm, 2–6pm. Closed Sunday.

Amira is by far the classiest candle shop in town. It's in an obscure location (near to the Sidi Ghanem Industrial Estate) but there are a few other places near here that you might want to visit as well (Akkal, La Medina, Mia Zia). Amira candles are renowned internationally and grace many a romantic Moroccan setting. They come in an assortment of shapes, sizes and colours so you'll almost certainly find something you'll like.

**Art de la Table, 57 Rue Ibn Aicha, Gueliz.**
Tel: 0 44 43 64 15 boutique1@wanadoo.net.ma
Open: 9am–1pm, 3.30–7.30pm. Closed Sunday.

Need some stylish tableware? Look no further. Art de la Table has been serving customers for two years with everything table-based and beyond. Plates, bowls, teacups, egg cups, soap dishes, vases, spice dishes, bowls, pots and other colourful bits and bobs in glass, porcelain and *tadelakt* fill this cute space.

**Artisan El Koutoubia , 54 bis, Fhel Chidmi Mouassine, Medina.**
Tel: 0 44 44 46 09 artkoutoubia@hotmail.com
Open: 9am–6pm daily

Artisan El Koutoubia is an organized and pretty little lamp shop that may appeal to those who prefer not to indulge in base haggling for illumination. The styles on display are similar to many in

the souks but the finish seems to be a little more professional.

**Côte Sud, 39 Residence Akioud, Semlalia.**
Tel: 0 44 44 81 30
Open: 9am–6pm. Closed Sunday.

Part artisanal store, part cutesy gift shop, Côte Sud packs a multitude of things into its compact space. The emphasis is on giftstyle objects with a 'novel' twist: pens, mirrors, *tajine* pots, Alessi kettles, decorated glasses, notebooks, silverware, candles, napkins, lamp shades, scents and soaps, etc.

**Interieur 29, B29 Rue Mansour Eddahbu, Gueliz.**
Tel: 0 44 43 31 12
Open 9.30am–12.15pm, 3.30–7pm. Closed Sunday, and Monday afternoon.

Pascal Colombeau and Hubert Aimetti design furnishings of all kinds in styles such as art deco and the more linear look known to some as 'colonial'. They work in wood, iron, alloys and all kinds of fabrics to create refined bedspreads, chairs, bowls, table sets, chests and mirrors among myriad other things. Everything is elegantly minimal and comes in *de rigueur* ethnic colours.

**Jamade, Riad Zitoun Jdid, 1 Place Douar Graoua, Medina.**
Tel: 0 44 42 90 42 www.ilove-marrakesh.com/jamade
Open: 10.15am–1.15pm and 3–8pm daily

Just along the well-traversed Riad Zitoun Jdid, Jamade is an elegant boutique that sells lots of attractive little accessories such as purses, slippers, jewellery, plates, handbags, candles and other knick-knacks. Everything is made locally and has a trendy slant.

**Lun'Art Gallery, 24 Rue Moulay Ali, Gueliz.**
Tel: 0 44 44 72 66 lunart@iam.net.ma
Open:10am–12.30pm, 4–8pm. Closed Sunday.

Lun'Art has been run by Luciano (Italian) and Said (Moroccan) for 10 years and is well known in town. Luciano is the designer, and his furniture has been increasingly in demand since he opened, not only by the general public but also by props specialists (his work has appeared in locally filmed movies such as *The Mummy* and *Kundun*). Larger products (e.g. garden furniture) are on display outside while the rest is shown around two big rooms inside the main building. There's a large ethnic and antique slant with such objects as Maori tables, Moroccan chairs and Balinese sculptures up for grabs.

**Maison de Bali, 61 Rue de Yougoslavie, Passage Ghandouri 34-35, Gueliz.**
Tel: 0 44 43 63 12 www.maisondebali.com
Open: 9am–7pm. Closed Sunday.

No prizes for guessing what this place specializes in. Aside from smart and expensive Balinese furnishings, however, Maison de Bali also stocks Moroccan goods and items from places such as Laos as well as Turkey and other European countries. Some pieces here are predictable, some imaginative, others irresistible. There's an especially good line in beds, tables and funky lamps. A second store can be found at 165 avenue Mohammed V.

**Original Design, 47 Place des Ferblantiers, Bab El Mella, Medina.**
Tel: 0 65 47 05 82 Original_design_mrk@yahoo.fr
Open: 9am–noon, 2–7.30pm Wednesday; 9am–7.30pm Thursday–Sunday

A pretty jewel amid the rough and clangorous environs of the Place des Ferblantiers, Original Design is the creation of Mademoiselle Ibtissam Ait Daoud. She has fitted out this small but very sweet place with her choice of crockery, embroidered materials, mirrors, soaps, *tajine* pots, place-mats, candles and other lovely knick-knacks. Prices are very reasonable, she accepts commissions, and can export bulk buys to Europe if you get really carried away.

## POTTERY AND CERAMICS

**Pottery Souk, Boulevard du Golf, Souk Rbiaa, SYBA, Medina.**
Open: 8am–7pm daily

If it's traditional pottery you seek – decorated or plain – then this large, shop-lined boulevard souk is for you. *Tajine* pots, mini-Koutoubias, vases, flowerpots, decorative objects and such like are all stacked up outside the premises in higgledy-piggledy fashion. Some of the stores will be happy to let you see how *zellije* tables or *tadelakt* lamps are made, if you're interested.

## TRADITIONAL CLOTHING

**Azziza, Centre Commercial Liberté, Rue de la Liberté, Gueliz.**
Tel: 0 44 44 98 73
Open: 8am–12.30pm, 3–7.30pm daily

Azziza is a Moroccan designer who makes prêt-à-porter garments for both men and women, although there is a bias towards ladies' wear. The shop stocks something for every occasion, from smart suits to leather jackets and casual *djellabas*. A lot of Azziza's designs are high quality if stylistically ordinary, but there are some experimental gems to be found.

**Galerie Birkemeyer, 169 Rue Mohammed El Bekal, Gueliz.**
Tel: 0 44 44 69 63 www.iam.net.ma/birkemeyer
Open: 8.30am–12.30pm, 3–7.30pm Monday–Saturday;
9am–12.30pm Sunday

A large store just off the Boulevard Zouktouni famed for its
selection of leather and suede clothing and accoutrements. The
staff look on somewhat balefully while you rummage through
everything from jackets, trousers, handbags, luggage and non-
leather items such as scarves and shirts. Not especially funky, and
not overly cheap, but the quality is good.

**La Maison du Kaftan Morocain, 65 Rue Sidi El Yamani,**
**Mouassine, Medina.**
Tel: 0 44 44 10 51
Open: 8am–7pm daily

As the name suggests, this shop specializes in traditional kaftans.
In fact, if you can't find the kaftan you're looking for in here, then
it probably exists only in your own mind, or in fashion haunts
such as Kulchi or Riad Tamsna. The shop front leads into a vast
room around which are hung kaftans of all colours and sizes;
antique kaftans, Berber kaftans – even magic kaftans! There are
also other traditional accessories such as *baboush*, chemises and
pantaloons, for both men and women.

# play...

Marrakech might be a little underwhelming in the sightseeing department, but the additional range of activities it has to offer is more than compensatory, certainly if you're willing to venture outside the city.

The more actively inclined can ascend Mount Toubkal, hike around the nearby Atlas Mountains, go wind-surfing in Essouira, or even ski and snowboard if conditions are right (the best times are between January and March). Less demanding but just as much fun to try are the city's horse-riding schools, and the go-karting and quad-biking courses.

Sports enthusiasts might enjoy a round or two of golf (there are three courses that host domestic and international championships), or perhaps some tennis, pigeon shooting, swimming or squash. Head out towards the desert and camel-riding, dune-climbing and 4x4 exploration safaris become an option. If you prefer spectator status you can catch a football game at the El Harti stadium.

Then there's the city's expansive spa and *hammam* scene. A *hammam* is a traditional form of deep-cleaning in Morocco. It consists of being steamed and washed down with black soap then thoroughly drubbed by a muscular man or woman sporting a mitt with a Brillo-pad-like texture (*gommage*). This is some-

times followed (depending on the type of *hammam* you book) by the application of lavender, rose water, a face mask or shampoo. Marrakech is becoming synonymous with beauty treatments and new spas offering a multitude of treatments are springing up all over. You can go and stay in them or just pop in for an hour or two to pamper yourself before dinner.

As a city Marrakech can be pretty hectic and if you are staying for longer than three days it might be nice to get out of the city to see somewhere else or just to relax in the countryside. Three different places immediately spring to mind. Firstly the Kasbah du Toubkal (see page 46); set in the shadow of Jebel Toubkal, the highest mountain in the High Atlas, the Kasbah is set in a stunning location with spectacular views – reached by a drive through the orchards of Asni. Go and have lunch, visit a real Berber village, wander the mountain trails or simply relax with a *hammam*.

The Kasbah Agafay (see page 44) is one of the few places that allows visitors to use their pool. Offering cooking courses, massage treatments and total relaxation in indulgent style make it worth the trip. At only 20km from Marrakech it is easy to reach.

Thirdly, La Roseraie in Ouirgane is a hotel with a pool, a professional spa, horse-riding and trekking. Slightly further out of Marrakech it is set in the calm and stillness of the High Atlas.

Marrakech and Morocco has so much to offer visitors it seems a pity not to make the most of it.

## COOKERY SCHOOLS

Morocco's natural pantry is a real joy, fresh fruit and vegetables are everywhere. If you wander the earthier side of the Medina the smells of fresh herbs and mint fills the air – if you head outside of the city in the autumn the aroma of apples and pears pervades. Mixed with a unique form of cuisine it is not surprising that some of Marrakech's better hotels have set up cookery schools.

**Dar Liqama, Douar Abiad, Palmeraie.**
Tel: 0 44 33 16 97 darliqama@menara.ma

In October and November this becomes the home of the internationally renowned Rhodes School of Cuisine. The kitchen is perfect for hosting small groups for intense courses.

**Kasbah Agafay, Route de Guemassa, Km 20.**
Tel: 0 44 36 86 00 www.kasbahagafay.com

Set in a stunning Kasbah with beautiful views over the desert, fields and the High Atlas make it a stunning location for a cookery school. The small kitchen garden provides all the fresh vegetables, fruits and herbs that you might possibly need. Go for the day or spend a couple of days staying here in luxury.

**La Maison Arabe, 1 Derb Assehbe, Bab Doukkala, Medina.**
Tel: 0 44 38 70 10 www.lamaisonarabe.com

This exclusive Medina hotel has a cookery school based out in the Palmeraie for the use of its guests. Coupled with a swimming pool it can be a therapeutic day out of relaxed cookery followed by reclining next to the pool.

## FOOTBALL

Football has always been a popular sport in the Arab world, with Middle-Eastern and North African teams regularly performing well in the World Cup and the African Nations Cup. it's certainly a popular sport in Marrakech, to the point where some people's only grasp of the English language will be a cheerful recitation of the names of a few Premier League fotball teams. The top local team is Kawab (KAC), although they never seem to fare particularly well  in the national league.

**El Harti Stadium, Jnane El Harti, Gueliz.**
Tel: 0 44 42 06 66

A 15,000-capacity stadium that acts as home ground for Kawab and also Najim. It's not glamorous and there aren't many facilities, but it's fondly regarded by the locals. Tickets are usually sold on the day of the game.

## GOLF

Golf in Morocco is surprisingly popular, and there are no fewer than three international courses located just outside the city. Courses are generally easy to get on to and relatively cheap compared with European prices – green fees start at around 300dh, caddies around 90dh. Of course, the weather is more or less guaranteed 300 days of the year.

**Golf d'Amelkis, Route de Ouarzazate, Km 12, Marrakech.**
Tel: 0 44 40 44 14
Open: 8am–4pm daily in summer; 8am–2pm daily in winter

Amelkis is the newest kid on the block and it shows. It's the best-looking course around (designed by Cabell B. Robinson) and boasts an elegant and relaxing clubhouse and professional on-site shop which sells everything from tees to T-shirts. Clubs cost 200dh per bag. A round will set you back 450dh and caddies can be hired.

**Palmeraie Golf Palace, Palmeraie.**
Tel: 0 44 30 10 10 www.pgp.co.ma
Open: 7am–7pm daily

Designed by international maestro Robert Trent Jones, this is the pride and joy – and the principal *raison d'être* – of the vast PGP estate. It's a classic American-style course with seven lakes, lots of palms and a very nice clubhouse and restaurant. Lessons can be arranged, and clubs can be rented for 25dh each or 250dh for the whole bag. Eighteen holes will set you back 450dh with a whole day on the course stretching you to 600dh. For ultimate decadence a local caddy can be arranged for 80dh.

**Royal Golf Club, Ancienne Route de Ouarzazate Km 2, Marrakech.**
Tel: 0 44 40 98 28 Royal_golf@iam.net.ma
Open: sunrise–sunset daily in summer; 9am–2.30pm daily in winter

The oldest and most regal of courses in Marrakech, this quite flat course is set in a dense forest of cypress, eucalyptus and palm trees, and is overlooked by the Atlas Mountains. Many of Morocco's more famous visitors have had a game here and lessons are given all year round. The clubhouse, new sports shop and bar have been recently constructed, offering a cool drink in the shade. Green fees are cheaper, costing 400dh for the day while the price of a caddy remains the same. Clubs cost 250dh for a bag.

# HORSE-RIDING

Marrakech has a variety of places where you can jump into the saddle. They are professionally run even if some look very basic, usually offering lessons, hacking and jumping, and catering for children as well as adults. All the places listed have paddocks of differing sizes, but also suggest trips around the countryside or into the mountains. The countryside directly surrounding Marrakech is not incredibly exciting, so you might like to arrange for the stables to meet you with horses in the mountains. Most stables will offer you trekking options with accommodation so you can spend up to four or five days riding outdoors.

**Cavalier Ranch, Route de Fes, Km 14, Marrakech.**
Tel: 0 62 61 22 51 cavalierranch@menara.ma
Open: 8.30am–7pm. Closed Monday.
Prices: Horses 100dh per hour, 600dh per day

Run by the oddly charming Gallaoui, this place is a little further out but worth it. The horses are Berber and Arabic; you can trot or jump around the paddocks, go out around the local villages or organize a longer-distance trip into the mountains or the desert (which includes food and accommodation).

**Club Equestre de la Palmeraie, Palmeraie Golf Palace, Palmeraie.**
Tel: 0 44 36 87 93 www.pgp.co.ma
Open: 8am–noon, 3–8pm daily in summer; 8am–noon, 3–6pm daily in winter
Prices: horses 150dh per hour, 800dh per day; ponies 50dh per 15mins, 90dh per hour.

The Golf Palace's stables are relatively small but probably the prettiest of the lot. There's a paddock that's used mainly for beginners and children, while accomplished riders can roam around the desert villages of the Palmeraie. The Palace has many other facilities nearby, including a hotel should you want to spend some more time here.

**La Roseraie, Ouirgane.**
Tel: 0 44 43 91 28/9

La Roseraie is a country hotel with horse-riding facilities located 60km from Marrakech (in the Ouirgane Valley). The advantage of coming all the way here is that you are already in the foothills of the Atlas Mountains with easy access to forests, reserves, hamlets and Berber villages where you can ride and trek. Horses can be ridden by the hour or you can disappear into the countryside for up to five nights, staying at Berber houses en route. The hotel has plenty of pleasant rooms, a fine restaurant, a full health spa and 50 acres of garden to relax in.

**Royal Club Equestre de Marrakech, Route d'Amizmiz, Km 4, Marrakech.**
Tel: 0 44 38 18 49
Open: 8am–noon, 2–6pm. Closed Monday.

This state-run stable is perhaps the main centre in town – it's certainly the most official. There are a couple of large paddocks here and several different types of pedigree horse to choose from. It offers individual lessons or will organize treks of varying lengths to suit. The trainers are professional and national competitions are held here occasionally. Prices start from 150dh per hour for a horse while children can get a 15-minute pony ride for 15dh.

## QUAD BIKING AND KARTING

### Atlas Karting, Route De Safi, Marrakech.
Tel: 0 64 19 05 37/0 61 23 76 87
www.ilovemarrakesh.com/atlaskarting or atlas_karting@yahoo.fr
Open: 8am–7pm daily

Atlas Karting is run by a pro Frenchman by the name of Gerard. It offers a challenging and fun-packed course that karters of all levels are welcome to try out (lessons and seminars are available). Day trips are also available that allow enthusiasts to get to grips with both quads and karts (1,900dh). There is a snack bar and hotel on site and quads, camels and horses are all on offer as well. A kart starts at 100dh for 10 minutes, while camels can be hired at 280dh for an hour.

### Mega-Quad Excursions, Route d'Amizmiz, Km 6.
Tel: 0 44 38 31 91/0 61 21 69 24 www.quadmaroc.com
Open: 8am–7pm daily

This is a neat little place with plenty of well-maintained quads, a tented restaurant on-site for lunches and special events, and a course that stretches across the local countryside. Trips to the mountains and the desert are available, starting at 2,000dh per day including lunch, and going up to 15,000dh. This pays for a minimum of six quads for five days, including accommodation.

## SKIING

**Oukaimeden Ski Resort**
Information: 0 2 20 37 98

The place ski-buffs should head for is the city of Oukaimeden, 74km outside Marrakech and 3,273m above sea level. It's North Africa's largest ski resort, initially developed by the French and more recently surveyed by international resort planners who aim to improve the infrastructure. Lift passes are cheap, as is the equipment to hire, but an absence of snow can be a slight problem. Between mid-January and mid-February is the safest bet, although the views are great all year round. In good conditions there are up to 20km of runs, the longest of which is 3km. Donkeys can be hired to access terrain not served by lifts, which opens up some impressive steeps and chutes. Otherwise ski touring is available including an ascent/descent of Jebel Toubkal, North Africa's highest mountain.

## SPAS AND HAMMAMS

**Bains de Marrakech, 2 Derb Sedra, Bab Agnaou, Medina.**
Tel: 0 44 38 14 28
Open: 9am–8pm daily

Bains de Marrakech, annexed to the delightful Riad Mehdi (see page 60), is one of the only places in town to offer extensive spa services in a non-corporate environment. Set in a *riad*, it boasts a delightful relaxation courtyard, and dark, scented corridors off which are located various treatment rooms. You can get everything here from a facial and a feisty *hammam gommage,* to a four-hand massage and French manicure. There are also some luxurious bathing options, including one that involves milk, orange flowers, sensual oils and rose petals; two sunken baths positioned next to each other mean you can indulge alone or with someone else. Day spas (3 hrs) and weekend packages are also available with prices starting at 70dh for a *hammam* up to 400dh for a massage.

## Centre de Balneotherapie, Tikida Garden, Circuit de la Palmeraie, Palmeraie.
Tel: 0 44 32 95 95 www.marrakech-tikida.com

Tikida's spa centre provides a daily shuttle service to and from Marrakech town centre. It's a little way out in the Palmeraie but boasts plenty of treatments and a relaxing setting among lush gardens. Facilities include swimming pool, hydro-massages, algo-therapy, jet showers, massage, presso-therapy, facials, aerobics, fitness rooms, a traditional *hammam*, steam room and relaxation area. A beauty salon offers a hairdresser, manicures, pedicures and henna tattooing. All treatments and services for both beauty centre and spa are available à la carte or as packages. There are also tennis courts, volleyball, tabletennis and archery (at an additional charge) should you feel like doing something more energetic.

**Dar Attajmil, 23 Rue Laksour, off Rue Sidi El Yamami, Medina.**
Tel: 0 44 42 69 66 darattajmil@iam.net.ma
Prices: *hammam* 200dh; with massage 440dh

If you'd like a more intimate *hammam* experience, try Attajmil. The *riad* itself is small (four rooms) and the *hammam* at the top is also compact, but it's sizeable enough and the treatment is professional and rigorous, with all the right essential oils being used. Mint tea is included in the price, and the roof garden is a gorgeous place to sip it and unwind – day or night. They need at least 3 hours' notice to get the fire going and guests take preference, so booking ahead is essential.

**Hammam Nikhil, Zohor I, Ain Itti**
Open: 6am–9.30pm daily

Local *hammams* in Marrakech can sometimes be run-down or downright unpleasant. Others, however, are newer, and manage to create a good balance of decent scrub-down facility, cleanliness and high sociability factor. Nikhil is one such. It's basic – think bright lights and shiny tiled floors – but cheap and clean and a great way of getting a direct insight into local social customs (many Marrakchi come here principally for a chinwag). As is customary, Nikhil has separate male and female sections and offers basic services from 7dh.

**Les Jardins de la Medina, 21 Rue Derb Chtouka, Kasbah, Medina.**
Tel: 0 44 38 18 51 www.lesjardinsdelamedina.com
Open: 8.30am–8.30pm daily
Prices: *hammam*, *gommage* and 30-minute massage 350dh

Les Jardins de la Medina doesn't have a spa complex as such, but does possess a *hammam* (downstairs near the swimming pool) and a health and beauty suite up on the roof, which offers haircuts, massages, facials and other assorted treatments. It's a little smaller than other *hammams* and as the hotel's guests obviously take preference, it's worth a phone call in advance.

### Le Spa du Palmeraie Golf Palace, Les Jardins de la Palmeraie, Palmeraie.
Tel: 0 44 30 10 10 www.pgpmarrakech.com
Open: 10am–9pm daily; Prices: massage 250–450dh, waxing 50–300dh, hydrotherapy 150–300dh

The Palmeraie Golf Palace is one of those sprawling hotel complexes that we wouldn't necessarily recommend staying at, but equally wouldn't discourage the use of their facilities. The spa here is inevitably commercial and boasts an extensive range of treatments (massage, hydrotherapy, waxing, saunas, *hammam*, jacuzzi, face masks etc. all available à la carte or as packages). In combination with the 18-hole golf course, a horse-riding paddock (with ponies for children), restaurants, bars and assorted other convenient distractions, it makes a good place to spend a lazy day. Massages start at 250dh.

### Sport e Bien, Residence Dalia, Avenue Yacoub El Mansour, Gueliz.
Tel: 0 44 30 39 23
Open: 8am–9pm daily

Sport e Bien is part of a larger complex along Yacoub El Mansour, a main artery that stretches off Mohamed V. It functions as gymnasium, beauty centre and health spa, offering a range of services from saunas and swimming to massages and facials. There is a *hammam*, a range of classes (karate, dance, step, etc.) and a hairdressing salon, too. The pristine interior has a professional if slightly corporate feel, but services are good, staff are friendly and eager to help, and it's easy to get to.

## SWIMMING

Finding somewhere decent to swim is not all that easy in Marrakech. There aren't very many public swimming pools and those connected to hotels and villas and are often only for guests. Places such as the Palmeraie Golf Palace, Jardins de la Koutoubia and Hotel El Andalous have been known to let lunchers use their pools for a fee (usually between 100–150dh), and some of the spas listed above (for example, Sport e Bien) have pools. The following two public spots may prove useful although they are open only in summer and Islamic custom dictates they are heavily male-orientated: it is perhaps best for women to avoid them unless they wish to be continuously ogled.

### Piscine El Koutoubia, Rue Abou El Abbass Essebti, Medina.

Tel: 0 44 38 68 64. Open: 9am–noon and 3–6pm from second week of June until first week of September. Closed Tuesday. Admission: 5dh

### Piscine Sidi Youssef Ben Ali, Avenue El Mederisa, Quartier Sidi Youssef Ben Ali.

Tel: 0 44 40 21 35
Open: 9am–noon and 2–5pm daily (July and August only)
Admission: 5dh

# TREKKING

The High Atlas begin just 50km from Marrakech, making it easy to hire a taxi and head out to the mountains for a day or as long as you like. The best time to go is in the spring when the valleys are filled with wild flowers, or in the autumn when the summer temperatures have died down and the fruit harvests take place. Trek from village to village soaking up the traditional Berber hospitality and legendary bartering skills or just walk through the quiet solitude that the mountains offer.

An ascent of Toubkal takes two days and affords the most amazing views at the summit. The best expeditions to the desert offer unique insights into how the nomadic people subsist, and allow you to explore the barren landscape and experience its colour as well as its loneliness.

**Bivouac Erg Laabidlia, Centre M'hamid.**
Tel: 0 44 84 80 88/0 61 55 53 69 erglaabidlia@yahoo.fr

Run by the friendly Naji Labaalli, this place is located in what feels like the last place on earth – M'hamid. It's only worth contacting them if you've got a minimum of three days as they'll arrange for you to come from Marrakech to M'hamid, a day's journey, from whence you have access to the desert. Naji owns desert *bivouacs* in Shakaga, which come equipped with cooks,

showers, lavatories, etc., and can organize walks, dune-climbs, camel rides, 4x4 tours and so on. Camels are 300dh per day, Jeeps 1,000dh per day, *bivouacs* 230dh per night (including lunch, tent and breakfast).

### Destination Evasion, Villa el Borj, Rue Khalid Ben Oualid, Gueliz.
Tel: 0 44 44 73 75/0 61 08 44 39
www.destination-evasion.com

Frenchman Pierre Yves Marais has been running excursions in Marrakech for five years, and knows his way around. He is able to tailor itineraries for groups or individuals ranging from a day trip to a week-long sojourn that takes in relaxed sightseeing, trekking through mountains and sleeping overnight in the desert.

### Kasbah du Toubkal, Imlil, High Atlas.
Tel: 0 44 48 56 11
www.kasbahdutoubkal.com

The Kasbah du Toubkal (see page 46), located next door to the village of Imlil, is a perfect starting-point for the ascent of Mount Toubkal. Staying here is a beautiful way to spend a few days and a great start and end to the arduous Toubkal climb or other walking and climbing options. All climbs and treks can be arranged through the Kasbah staff; prices range from 25dh per half-day trek to 200dh per person for a full ascent, all with guides, cooks, mules, accommodation and drinks (if required).

### Rak Express, 221 Avenue Mohammed V, Gueliz.
Tel: 0 61 42 23 49
Rak-express@menara.ma

Moroccan owner Mohamed Helgane has worked for many tour companies and seems to have an infinite number of quality contacts on his books. He can take care of everything from hotel reservations to car hire, but also arranges day tours around the city (300dh per full day/200dh per half-day), mountain tours, desert journeys, camel-trekking, Berber trails (620dh including lunch) and day trips.

# info...

## CUSTOMS

Marrakech is a Muslim city, and no matter how laid-back it feels at times it is still staunchly Islamic at heart. Certain rules should thus be followed, the main ones being to dress conservatively in religious places (and in people's homes), and if you would like to photograph someone, ask them first – women especially. Doing so should avoid causing offence. Many Muslims drink, most seem to smoke and drugs are also available, although penalties are severe for even the slightest drug offence.

## DANGERS

Marrakech has an undeserved reputation for hassle. Stories abound of visitors being badgered from the moment they arrive in the country, though in truth those days are long past. This is thanks to the Tourist Police, set up in 1999 to quickly remove and reproach anyone caught giving undue or unwanted attention to a foreigner. You'll still be approached by persistent beggars and hard-sell hustlers, but they are generally easy to shrug off – a knowing smile works better than a stern face. If they do become overly persuasive just mouth the word 'police' and they should melt away. Failing that, cause a fuss and someone will usually appear to resolve the situation (Moroccans lose their temper easily but it hardly ever leads to violence and is just as quickly forgotten about). Also underserved is the city's reputation for being an unsafe place for foreign women. Many female ex-pats who have lived here for years speak only of respectful treatment by Moroccan men. Of course there are oglers and the occasional sly commentators, but these can be easily ignored. Again, if you do find yourself in a compromising situation, follow the advice above. Pickpockets also sometimes operate in crowded areas – such as the Jemaa El Fna – so keep an eye on personal belongings.

## MONEY

The *dirham* is the unit of currency for Morocco. It is possible to buy them in the UK (and elsewhere outside Morocco) although immigration may confiscate them since they prefer their currency to stay in the country. It's better to use

ATMs while there (there are enough around to make it easy) or bring travellers' cheques. At the time of writing, £1 = 16dh, €1 = 11dh, 1US$ = 10dh.

## TELEPHONES

All numbers given in this book exclude the international dialling code but include the Marrakech city code. To call any number from Marrakech simply dial as written. To call Marrakech from the UK, dial 00 212 followed by 44 for Marrakech. To telephone from a public phone look out for the coin-operated tele-boutique booths (marked by a large blue and white sign) or the orange card-operated phones. Cards can be bought from newsagents or post offices.

## TIPPING

Tips in restaurants should be around 5–10% depending on the level of service. For taxis, if the driver gives you a fair price and use's the meter give him a decent tip or simply round up; for those that don't use the meter give them nothing extra.

## TRANSPORT

There is public transport outside the Medina (mainly buses and the occasional horse-drawn caleche) but it's much easier and more convenient to get around by taxi. Taxis come in two types: petit and grand. The petit is the main mode of transport for short distances (i.e. within the city). They are small, light-brown cars (often Fiats) that, just in case, have the word 'Petit' stencilled onto their roof-racks. They are ubiquitous and inexpensive, with a ride from the Medina to Gueliz, for example, costing around 10dh. However, half the drivers are the biggest chancers in town. Many honest ones will simply click on a meter, but many will claim it's broken or just ignore you if you ask. Two things can happen here: either they are honest and genuinely don't operate with a meter (and will simply charge you the correct fare), or they will try and overcharge you. It's a perennial frustration but often best simply to hail another cab if a driver refuses to meter the ride. Minimum fare is 5dh. Grand taxis are bigger, estate-style cars and mainly used for large groups or long journeys out of town.

# index

# index